Teaching the
SLOW LEARNING CHILD

Teaching the
SLOW LEARNING
CHILD

BY

MARION FUNK SMITH

In collaboration with
ARTHUR J. BURKS

*Lt. Col., United States Marine Corps Reserve;
Wartime President, Aptitude Board,
Marine Barracks, Parris Island, S. C.*

HARPER & BROTHERS, NEW YORK

Library of Congress catalog card number: 53–11862

Contents

v

58296

Preface

THE purpose of this book is to acquaint the public with those children in our schools with I.Q.'s of 50 to 89 whom we have called the "educable retarded." It is the belief of the writers that more could and would be done for these children if people knew the facts about them. There are many mistaken beliefs prevalent concerning the abilities of this group and the manner of educating them. While many communities have an adequate program of education there are some districts which make no allowance for them and others which believe in the old system of accentuating craft instruction only.

In this book my collaborator and I have attempted to bring out the human side of the picture. These boys and girls are not mentally deranged or incompetent. Comparing their minds to an engine we would say they have a slower dynamo than has the average child but it is a good dynamo. They do, however, need specialized methods and techniques and a program suited to their needs. This program should be a realistic, meaningful presentation of the academic work which will equip them to handle their daily tasks. It should include, in junior high school, training in home economics and shop in addition to academic subjects, physical education, and character building. In senior high school it should include preparation for job training as well as a continuation in the junior high school subjects.

My theories about educating the retarded are the result of diversified teaching experiences. After graduation from the University of Pennsylvania, where I majored in psychology and English, I taught for four years in a special school. Here I handled all six departmental groups in academic subjects. From there I went to an elementary school where I taught a segregated special class for three years. Here the class came and left in a bus and were socially and emotionally separated from the rest of the school. They did not participate in school activities on either an equal or an unequal footing. Next I taught English in a junior high school where I had six seventh-grade classes. The retarded section was called the Junior Vocational Group. They were not segregated but joined the others and were simply "another" seventh-grade section with each subject tailored to fit their needs. For four years I was the assistant executive secretary of a community center. During a Christmas vacation one year I taught for ten days at Sleighton Farms at Wawa, Pennsylvania. This was to gain an insight into what happens to a girl who becomes a delinquent. Now I am teaching in a non-segregated elementary group in an elementary school. The term "non-segregation" is used because my present class is socially accepted by other children in the school and is not called "special," "opportunity," or "orthogenic backward" except in the records. The other children know that my pupils are boys and girls who have fallen behind in their work and need the individual attention possible in a smaller class. The class plays with the others, serves on the safety patrol with them, has representatives in the Red Cross group, and participates in May Day in the auditorium programs. Thus far the class has held its own in cooperative activities and done a creditable job.

In this book we have addressed our efforts to prospective teachers, teachers of average classes, new teachers in the field, and members of P.-T.A.'s. In addition we believe that the taxpayers might like to know something about these boys and girls, since more and more attention will be directed toward equalizing educational opportunities for them in the years to come.

From a teaching experience of over fifteen years, I have selected some particular children who give me the opportunity to disclose a wide range of classroom episodes, each with its own individual problem and its own individual solution.

These are my children, with their heartaches, their warmth, their need for love and understanding. Each one is a distinct personality, a citizen in the making. What kind of a citizen will each one be? The answer lies with all of us.

MARION FUNK SMITH

Collaborating Author's Comments

In 1943–44 I was lay president of the Aptitude Board, Marine Barracks, Parris Island, South Carolina. I was also Recruit Depot Training Officer with the rank of major. The Aptitude Board convened every Friday. I marched to the corner room in the Sick Bay. On the lawn, the steps, in the halls, and around the doors sprawled sturdy men in training uniform. I knew there would be about 130 of them. They had passed every physical phase for enlistment in the Marine Corps. They had all failed to make the grade in actual training.

For several weeks medical officers, surgeons, dentists, psychologists, and psychiatrists, all commissioned Navy personnel (Medical Corps, attached to the Marine Corps) had studied these men whose unfitness began to show during their first days of training. The medical officers recommended that they be discharged as unfit.

The men would have to explain, all the rest of their lives, why they had been discharged in wartime.

As lay president, with other members of the Aptitude Board explaining each individual's record and that individual facing me across a desk, I could approve the board's finding in each case, or return the recruit for more training. I seldom returned a man to the drill field. When I did, sooner or later he faced me again, over the same desk.

These unfit ones had never been rehabilitated. Their

march to public finding of unfitness must have begun in earliest childhood. Every last one could have been saved if caught in time.

They were the retarded. Mentally, emotionally, and spiritually, they were the slow learners who, grown up, could no longer be saved to useful integration, certainly not in the military. What a tremendous pool of lost man-power here, not for "cannon-fodder," but for citizenship. Could most of these men have been rehabilitated if noted in time?

After the war, during Special Education Week in Lancaster, Pennsylvania, I met Marion Funk Smith. I visited her class repeatedly, studied the children she was demonstrably rehabilitating. I convinced myself that she was doing the work that should be done in childhood for the slow. She was teaching 18 children yearly. My Aptitude Board had discharged 130 weekly. I did not research other branches of the Armed Services, nor delve deeply into the economic status of the adult retarded, beyond the discovery that they are often comfortably indigent, housed and fed by taxpayers.

Mrs. Smith's simple techniques, I felt, should be more widely known and used. A book should be written. I roughed out a chapter or two for her consideration. For one who did not claim to be a writer she did strange and awesome things to the copy. It became impossible to ascertain just which of us had written what. But the "I" of the narrative refers, of course, to Mrs. Smith.

That's true collaboration. This book is the result.

ARTHUR J. BURKS

Teaching the
SLOW LEARNING CHILD

I

Little Vegetable

I HELD up the flash card. I hoped none of the children or the visitor would see that my hand trembled. It did not tremble because I doubted, but because I knew. A single word appeared on my side of the card. The word was "jump." The same word appeared on the other side.

Facing me, to read the card, was small blond Carol, eight years old. She was spick and span in freshly ironed shirtwaist and dress. Her shoes were almost new. Her hair was beautifully combed. She was a little plump. Her eyes were gray, eager, confident.

Beside Carol sat ten-year-old Ned, my current teacher's helper. His small pointed face and dark eyes were as eager and confident as Carol's.

To my left, beyond the desk, sixteen other pupils watched and listened. Neither Carol nor Ned had ever had such an intent audience.

"Dzump," said Carol.

"Jump," I corrected. Ned said it just ahead of me: "Jump."

"Jump," said Carol.

The class applauded. I applauded with them. Never in her life had Carol been so proud. Ned was, if possible, even prouder, and in some ways he had a right to be.

I flashed another card on which appeared the word "down."

"Daoun," said Carol. I had repeated this word for Carol several times during the week. To my delight she corrected herself, before Ned or I could. "Down!" she said, in triumph.

I flashed other cards.

"Up," said one.

"Ap," said Carol.

"Boy."

"Boyn," said Carol.

"Run."

"Wun," said Carol.

I ran through a handful of flash cards. Not once did she exactly pronounce a word. Not once did she fail to know what the word was. Carol could *read*.

For fifteen years I had been teaching slow learners, the so-called retarded children, boys and girls. I had known many high points of inspiration and revelation in these years, but never one as completely satisfactory as this reading of Carol's.

Just a few years ago, a doctor had said to Carol's mother:

"Her I.Q. is forty-seven. She will never learn anything. The best you can hope for her is that she will occupy space. She will be a vegetable."

The mother did not disagree. She knew that laymen do not disagree with the pronouncements of experts. But she did not believe Carol's case to be hopeless. With an I.Q. of 47, Carol could not be sent to any public school in Pennsylvania, whose authorities require the education of boys and girls with I.Q. 50 and above.

Carol's mother loved her daughter. She did not feel herself disgraced that Carol had been sent to her. She did not regard Carol as a "visitation." She regarded this "little vegetable" of hers as a responsibility bestowed upon her by God.

Carol's father was gone, and the mother found herself in restricted circumstances. She could so easily have postponed sending Carol to the Child Development private school which handled children of I.Q.'s under 50. She didn't. She worked early and late for the money she needed. In the private school Carol found love and understanding. She responded. Of course she responded. Nobody stared at her there, nobody pointed.

After one year Carol's I.Q. was found to be 59. I am not an expert on intelligence quotients I have always left them to the experts. But could her I.Q. have been 47 one year and 59 the next, or could her medical examiners have been wrong both times? I do not know. The answer lies in checking and re-checking results of intelligence tests. But with a supposed I.Q. of 59, the teachers at the Child Development School became hopeful and Carol was sent to me. She came with the usual disparagements from every interested person but the school faculty and her mother, whose faith had never wavered.

The others said:

"She may possibly learn to do something useful with her hands. Even this is doubtful. Possibly she may learn simple social adjustments. Actually, she has no business in any classroom, anywhere, special or not. She can, at best, occupy space."

I did not believe this. I never believe people who run down my slow learners. And they are "mine" long before I see them. They are "mine" when I am told that they are coming. They are mine from the instant someone warns me that nothing can be done for them. The warning is always couched thus:

"This child has shown no ability to learn."

In fifteen years of dedication to the retarded I have found not one child who could not learn. I have found four, all teen-age boys, who *would* not learn. Their parents regarded the special class as a disgrace and a waste of time. The boys copied their parents' attitudes. Two now serve long terms in prison.

When I talked first with Carol my heart sank. Maybe, for the first time, the critics were right. Maybe, at last, here was a child who could not learn. But I would not allow myself to admit it. The 50 I.Q. mind is a fair mind. It is slow, that's all. I asked Carol questions, and she answered. I could no more understand the little blonde's speech than if she had been speaking Sanskrit. I felt sure she understood me, for she strained to answer. Her speech was just a jumble of sounds. Yet they had a familiar ring. I had heard this "dialect" before somewhere.

Ned walked up to the desk. I remembered. I had not been able to understand his speech, either, the year previous. I understood him now when he said:

"Let me talk with her, Mrs. Smith."

Without waiting, he began talking with Carol in her own "language." Once again I found Ned incomprehensible. But not Carol! I have never seen anyone, even in the dramatic day-to-day give-and-take of my class, blossom so quickly into flower. I have never known anyone to begin shining so quickly. Carol's hands shot out, palms forward. As if this odd gesture were part of her language, which Ned understood, Ned shot out his palms to meet Carol's.

Facing each other through, or between, the opposing palms, they chattered like two young immigrants from some country that never was. They laughed. Their faces were expressive of delight. Surely two people had never before become friends so quickly.

"What is she saying, Ned?" I asked.

Ned scarcely heard me, so intent on Carol was he. I touched him. He turned. I repeated the question. Slowly, then, Ned told me what she said. She was glad to be with other children. She did not say "other vegetables like me," but that is what she meant. In that instant Ned became my "co-teacher," the newest of many I had joyfully used through the years.

"Thank you very much, Ned," I told him. "We are happy to have her and want her to feel at home among us. You tell her that, too."

Carol nodded and smiled. She understood, even before Ned put my words into Carol's language. Who shall say that Carol's speech was not a language, at least a dialect? I did not understand Ned's interpretation or Carol's slow repetition of it

"Help Carol to say it as I said it, Ned," I instructed the boy.

He seemed to comply. I could not understand his words, but Carol understood them. Over and over, becoming more intelligible with each repetition, Ned repeated my simple words, Carol trying her best to follow her new friend out of her own word jungle. By the time both had tired of the lesson, I was able to understand a word or two of Carol's.

Now, months later, I could understand many words Carol said. The "little vegetable" was learning to read. I wanted to shout her triumph from my classroom window. Carol was never going to be restricted to helplessness in the world of adults while her slow mind atrophied with years. I knew this. In fifteen years many of my pupils had finished school and gone out into the world. I religiously maintained contact with them.

I held up another flash card.

"Mother," said Carol clearly.

I could have hugged her. I did. The hug she returned renewed me.

II

The Blue Hour

SCHOOL was finished for the day. My last child had smiled or hugged me and left for home. I sat alone behind my desk. I seldom hurried home. Staying after school had become almost a ritual, though I am averse to rituals generally, if slow learners are involved, since no two retarded children of my lengthy acquaintance have ever been enough alike to justify formulas for their education.

My ritual was precious to me. I recommend it, though it has never increased my salary. My hour, more or less, behind my desk, after school, became standard practice early in my life as a teacher. The first effort I made after the door had slammed for the last time that day, on the last boy or girl, was toward mental and physical relaxation. I needed both.

I came to school every morning at my peak of efficiency.

I left school every evening, if I permitted myself, feeling as if the day had aged me several years.

Each morning I was capable of whipping my world; each evening I had myself to whip. There were no easy answers to my problems.

Every child is a problem to the teacher. The average normal child, I.Q. from 90 to 110, is usually capable of helping the teacher to help him solve his problems. His mind is active, alert, more or less eager.

7

The child whose I.Q. is below 90, down to 50—where my lowest found their niches—must have help.

I rested for ten minutes, restoring the ravages of the day. I was no doctor, capable of treating the sick, no surgeon capable of delicate surgery, while maintaining an impersonal attitude. Every child of my classroom was as much my child as my own daughter.

My blue hour began this way:

I thought of Carol, since she was my latest child, and asked myself these questions: "Have I failed her today, in any way? Should I have done something for her, said something to her, that I did not do, did not say?"

In order to be sure of the answer, I pictured Carol in my memory of the day. She had come to school this morning with a smile. She had been immaculate. She had come all the way across town, by bus, *alone*. She had been doing this since she started in my class, because the class and I had given her the confidence that she could. Had I complimented her on her safe negotiation of fares, bus, streets? That was no longer necessary; she took bus trips for granted now. It was an old story. I closed my eyes and saw her dress again, her hair-do, her shoes. I saw her take her seat. I watched her through the day. I had, apparently, overlooked nothing. If I found I had, I noted it on the pad I pulled under my right elbow.

I dismissed Carol from my mind, though I did wonder what she and her proud, faithful mother talked about. Carol would tell me tomorrow, or one day the mother would visit me and comment. That was one good thing about my class. Since it was not labeled, nor referred to as a special class, my parents did come to class to watch the children at their work. It made me happy to be in a school so broad-minded and far-sighted that no one was segregated. My door was always open for parents. They came to my class without embarrassment.

I thought of Ned, then, and the sixteen other pupils who relied upon me for rehabilitation. Early in life, far too early, every one had discovered himself, herself, to be different, sometimes a little, sometimes a great deal. Faced with this difference, which far too many people were far too eager to point out and emphasize, slowly at first, unbelievingly at first, but faster as they became convinced of their difference, they withdrew inwardly, until their retreat from the days, and the dwellers in the days, became headlong. By the time they were old enough for school, most had crawled into the darkest depths of themselves and sought sanctuary from the world. The world—with knowing grins, pointed fingers, jeering words—encouraged them to retreat more deeply into their personal sanctuaries.

It was my duty to bring each one forth. I knew I could do it. I knew that there was at least one key to every childish inner sanctuary. It was my job to find it. If I failed to find it, the hunt would become gradually more difficult, the problem more difficult to solve. I never, all my teaching life, doubted I would find the right key for each boy and girl.

I never took anything for granted, though. I never took chances. I balanced my books with each child at the end of each day, exactly as if the child had been a bank, I the book-keeper.

Had John been untidy on arrival that morning? My pupils were noted for their good appearance. It was a thing to be noted for. I began, unobtrusively, to make good appearance a tenet of faith for each new pupil. It was the easiest, simplest thing in which the boy or girl could take pride.

That boy or girl needed something of which to be proud. Pride was part of the basic foundation for rehabilitation.

Had Peter pulled the braids of the little girl in the seat ahead of him? Had he twisted the arm of the smaller boy across the aisle to his left? If Peter pulled braids, and Peter were normal, a reprimand served, or the girl, or Peter, could be moved to another desk; but Peter was slow, frustrated; he must learn that strong boys did not pull girls' braids, and he must learn why. Explanations must be given Peter at his own level of understanding. That inner urge which impelled him to pull little girls' braids must be expelled from Peter's personality. It must be done without leaving scars, without leaving a vestige of itself. I knew how, or was learning how, to reach Peter. Every indication pointed to the fact that Peter craved recognition. I could rehabilitate any child I could reach. So why not Peter?

I could reach any child capable of thought; capable of being induced to think, and Peter could both think and analyze.

Peter had what seemed to be sadistic tendencies. I must lead him away from them. No prison must ever await Peter. I would never see his name in the headlines, read this kind of a quotation of Peter:

"I don't know what came over me. Everything went dark. I had the urge to kill. I could not help myself. My hands had a life of their own."

Peter was ten. My chances would have been better if he had come to me at eight, but I would succeed anyway at any age. It just became more difficult with growth and years.

The slow to learn become slower to learn, if dedicated teachers and parents do not intervene.

Peter, when he left me, would be too sure of himself in other ways, too proud, to have any urge to hurt any one. At his age, hurting someone else was a way of attracting attention to himself. Desire for attention was a deeply human urge. There were legitimate reasons for attracting attention, many of them, not always the same for boys and girls, seldom, indeed, the same for any two children.

Peter wanted to "be somebody." He did not want to be on relief, like his father. That made him different from Paul, whose father was also on relief; Paul, who believed that relief offered just the right security, and looked forward to it for himself.

Had I failed Peter in any way, today? Had I failed Paul?

If I had not, I dismissed their shadows until the next day. If I had, I made careful, complete notes, which would make sense when morning came. These notes gave me impetus for tomorrow's work with Peter, Paul, or Carol, or Jane.

Carefully I worked my way back in memory through every member of the class. George still snapped his fingers and called my name loudly—distracting the easily distracted attention of the rest—when he wished to ask a question, or leave the room, or visit with a classmate. More work was indicated here, with George, who seemed unable to help himself, and shook his head over his actually trivial shortcoming much more than I did. It was the nervousness behind his noise that was important. He lacked security. He must find it. I noted him for closer, more personal attention. One thing on the credit side of George's ledger was this: he liked to read so well that he wished to read faster, to race into more advanced readers than he was, as yet, capable of grasping. His urge was to come out, not retreat.

Mary, what about Mary? She was big for ten, fat, lovable, and always hungry. She sneaked food into her desk. She ate too much at home. But she did not eat, I was sure, as much, or as voraciously, as she had when she had come to me. Mary needed a lot of work in the diet department, always would. I made a note I had been making almost every day since Mary came to me. Academically Mary, with an I.Q. of 70, was slower than my 59 I.Q. Carol. I had had other Marys, other Carols, and this had always puzzled me. Thus I had come to the conclusion that the value of I.Q. tests lay chiefly in establishing the general grouping in which children belonged.

I went through all eighteen of my pupils. Eighteen, just about half the number of pupils teachers of normal children were required to handle at one time.

When satisfied that I had done everything possible for my small slow ones that day, I went home to my daughter, Glenna Mary, who has a rather high I.Q., which sometimes poses problems as difficult for her to solve, and her teachers to solve, as are Carol's, and mine with Carol.

My duties as a teacher did not require this daily recapitulation. But I was paid for it, maybe even overpaid, in coinage more valuable than is named in any teacher's pay-check. I cannot put that coinage into one word, or a few words, as parents of slow children will realize. I have to feel my way with words, as many as may be necessary, exactly as I feel my way into the dark recesses of new pupils' sanctuaries, to lead them forth into their rightful light.

I share that light with every child. It is payment heaped up, pressed down, and running over.

There were twenty-four movable desks in my classroom. One of the thoughts which made my blue hour blue was a kind of fantasy. One-fifth of the pupils attending the elementary schools of the United States, at any given moment in a school year, were like Carol, Mary, Jane, Peter, John, and George. I always saw this vast sweep of desks, at which shadows of boys and girls I would never know, were seated, and wondered if I were not somehow failing many, many thousands of these children.

It was a silly idea, of course, for what could just one teacher of the retarded do? If I had even reasonable success with my eighteen, I accomplished all that was expected of me.

Just the same, thought of that sea of desks intruded, down the years, into every daily blue hour, until I dismissed it by going home, where I lived a second life, not too vastly different from my life by day.

III

Walking Footballs

ALMOST all the children who come to me have been kicked around. Parents, probably the first to deny it, have kicked them around. They have sent them to different schools, different teachers. They have lost patience with them. They have said cutting things to them. Children who do not know when words are cutting can tell by the intonations of the voice. Dogs know, too, and few are as intelligent as the least mentally endowed of my pupils. Too many people regard the so-called retarded as they regard trees, alive, but more or less insensitive. They talk down to them, talk at them, talk about them in their presence, talk around them as if they were not there, deprecate openly their lack of mental speed.

The average retarded boy or girl is an exile not only in society, on the street, in the school, but in his own home. Too often a retarded child's parents say this to someone, while the retarded child listens, absorbing much more than he is ever credited for:

"I don't know what I ever did to deserve *this*."

If it is true that little pitchers have big ears, it is truer still that the ears of dull pitchers are biggest of all.

When a child comes to my class, if he has had any schooling at all, I know certain things about that child:

He has been the despair of his mother.

He has been the shame of his father.

He has attended too many schools.

He has been shunted from class to class.

He has been thumbed down by too many teachers, whom I cannot blame too much, since most teachers have little actual time, however deep their dedication, to devote to individuals. They can do well enough with normal children, who are able and eager to do something for themselves. They kick the dull normal child around, because they have no time to do otherwise. They by-pass him as a reader because he simply can not read at the level of his class; they have him read to show him up, or to symbolize to the class what is *not* acceptable; they promote him by "kicking him upstairs" to be rid of him.

The slow boy or girl, told often enough that he cannot learn, may not actually believe it, but may seem to because it is easier; and it is easier for the slow child to do the least thoughtful thing.

The slow boy is sent to some class where his hands can be trained; the slow girl where she can learn to sew, cook, or shop—or mix colors.

The instant a new child enters my class I know he has been kicked into it, sometimes literally. And this is true though he never, anywhere in my school or school district, or in my state, is the recipient of a harsh word. The kinder the principal, the parent, the teacher, the harder the toe of the invisible shoe.

And all because the dullest child *knows*.

He knows himself a stranger in his confusing world.

My first task is to convince him that he is no stranger. I convince him that I am his friend; a close friend. I cannot be closer without being a close relative—and yet, in a certain way, I can be. There is such a thing as being so close to something, a place, a wall, a person, that one has but a blurred image of it.

The average normal person has more of a blurred picture of the slow child than the slow child has of the world, and of his place in it.

So when a child comes to me he must first know that he is among friends, beginning with me, and including all other members of the class, who he quickly learns are his mental brethren.

A child approaches me diffidently. My first task is to erase, on a sound psychological basis, his diffidence. If he were normal he might himself overcome it by exercising his reason. But parents and schoolmates have convinced him that his reasoning powers are of little value. He accepts their judgment as final and correct, withdrawing into himself instead of rebelling, poking his head out, like a fearful rodent out of a cat-watched burrow.

A child approaches me arrogantly, strutting. He expects to be stepped on, kicked, and believes his only hope of survival is to step first, kick first. He is blood brother to the child who cringes openly, not in disguise. I have a general idea of how to handle the cringing child, the arrogant child; but each child is an individual: he can not be pigeonholed. No two cringing children or arrogant children are alike. I find the cause of the cringing and the arrogance as quickly as I can—to cut short actual suffering—and remove the cause.

A child approaches me sullenly. I find out why he, or she, is sullen. Sometimes it is easy, sometimes difficult, but when the cause is found, rehabilitation is simple and certain.

I wish to emphasize one thing I have learned in fifteen

years of dealing with the slow learner: *it takes so little to bring the child forth from his personal sanctuary*. Once he exits, or even pokes out his head, it takes little—beyond love, understanding, encouragement—to help him to find himself in the world, able to fight his own battles, shoulder his own burdens.

The slow child is born with two strikes against him; but if he is sent to me, and strikes out, it is not his fault; it is *mine,* and I must face an accounting somewhere, sometime, beginning in my own heart and conscience. If I were the father or mother of such a child I would say exactly the same thing about myself; but it is not the prerogative of a teacher to criticize parents. I make sure of my own lack of prejudice by not researching parents beyond information that comes my way when parents visit the school.

There are unnaturally pale boys and girls in almost every normal class. There are unnaturally thin normal boys and girls. There are hesitant boys and girls. There are wide-eyed, sunken-eyed, dull-eyed, fearful-eyed, boys and girls in every normal class. But boys and girls who come to my class always seem, at first, to be paler, thinner, more hesitant, more wide-eyed, sunken-eyed, dull-eyed, or fearful-eyed than normal children.

The difference is simple. Normal children find life filled with problems. So do the slow children. But for the slow child, less equipped to meet challenges generally, the problems are more difficult, the obstacles greater.

I have often wondered how the average normal boy or girl would face it if mistaken consistently for a retarded child and treated as so many retarded children are treated by the unthinking? I use the term "unthinking" advisedly, because no thinking person could possibly push the slow child around as case histories indicate that most slow children are pushed around.

Why should children who find obstacles difficult be faced with higher, harder obstacles? It is a paradoxical thing and must not be allowed to continue.

I make every child feel at home, as much as a child can possibly feel at home in a schoolroom; the "class family" helps me do this, indeed does the most about it, because its members quickly learn that feeling at home is the beginning of self-realization.

Next, I recognize the new pupil, not only for what he is, what he seems to be, but what I know he will become, given a chance.

The child who comes to me has ceased to be a football—family, school, communal, or political. From here on *I* do the kicking, until the child is able to kick for itself instead of being kicked. I do battle with anybody who treats one of my retarded children as if he, or she, were inferior. I make sure my pupils know I will fight for them; I have found this the surest way to inspire them to fight for themselves.

Maybe, to some extent, all of us are footballs; but most of us can at least bounce. Usually the retarded child has been so deflated by life, from his first realization of his difference on, that he does not even bother to bounce.

No child in my class remains deflated longer than it takes me to recognize his outstanding ability. It may be almost too small for even me to see, but when I see it I mention it to him, her, and to the class family.

I like to be recognized for my worth. So do you. We can both exist, after a fashion, without such recognition; but to the slow child *recognition is life itself.*

Recognition is one of the first bricks laid in the foundation I help the slow child to build under his firming feet.

The classroom quickly takes the place, in the heart of the slow boy or girl, of the personal sanctuary he has created within himself. The child exits from himself into the classroom.

The classroom must send him forth into wider spheres of activity, adequately equipped to perform his share in them.

IV

My First is for Retention

THE reading level of the average normal child, with an I.Q. of 90 to 110, is much lower than the average normal adult thinks. An excellent test of this statement can be made by each reader of this book. Sit back and read it aloud. I use the simplest of words. I want to make sure I am understood. My responsibility to parents and educators who read, and who, God willing, find the techniques useful, so that slow learners are allowed to learn, lies heavily on my shoulders. I allow myself no mistakes.

Does the reader stumble over any of the words? Does he have to look at a few of the longer words letter by letter, sounding the syllables in his mind, before he can be sure he knows the word—while whoever listens strains for him to find it, so that the reading will sound coherent?

This stumbling manner of reading I must erase from my slow ones. My task is easier, though it is never what I can call easy, if they come to me before they are eight years of age, and before they have mislearned elsewhere. In no wise do I suggest criticism of other teachers here. I must repeat that the teacher of the average normal class always has too many pupils, never has a chance to reach individuals. There simply is not enough time or human endurance. But the slow learner suffers.

I prefer children to come to me for their primer or pre-primer work. A year or two make little difference at this age. If it takes an extra year with any child, it matters little to me, to the school, or to the community; but it matters vitally to the child. The greater portion of life—I would hesitate to say how great a portion it appears to be—is blanked out for the person who cannot read. *The retarded child can learn, if not placed under undue pressure.*

The powers of retention of slow learners are low. One must labor to build memory into the retarded. It can be done. I have done it for years. It is a slow process. But success is usually lasting. There are always exceptions, I suppose. This does not seem remarkable. I know I do not remember everything I learned in elementary school, high school, or college. Many examinations I once passed easily I could not now pass without intensive "cramming."

I must repeat things with the retarded. I must keep them repeating. And repetition must not be allowed to wash out meaning. An excellent example of what I mean is the manner in which many people recite the Lord's Prayer. The words, from much repetition, have lost their meaning. The prayer is not felt, not lived. That can happen in class, with almost fatal results.

My first step in avoiding this is to make sure that I, myself, continue to feel and live the words I have lived and felt for fourteen years. Of course it is not easy to be a child, a retarded child, or to reach the retarded child. If it were easy I would be as fresh at night as I am when I reach school each morning. It takes something out of the most dedicated teacher. For this very reason the retarded child may be slighted—*so slighted as to be lost to the family, the com-*

munity, and the nation, so that he becomes an indigent instead of a producer.

Take the flash cards, simple cards on which simple words appear, sometimes with illustrative pictures. I take my pupils through these cards time after time, until they know the words on sight. Then I shuffle the cards, and do it again, and again. Then I ask each child to tell me what he believes each word to mean. I ask him to run through a page or two of some book in which the word appears, possibly more than once, and find the word, show it to me. I have him find other words, which he may not know, but which have the same beginning or ending as the word I am fixing in his evasive memory. I use every means I have learned over the years to help that child to help himself retain words, a given word.

My class is not graded. Pre-primer, primer, the first, second, third, and fourth grades, are taught in "Mrs. Smith's Class." When I am working with the first-, second-, third-, or fourth-grade reading levels (always I accent reading, though collateral academic subjects are, of course, studied equally thoroughly) I encourage, in that I do not discourage, all pupils who read easily at lower levels to participate in the reading at the higher levels, by looking on and listening. I have found that such listeners, who in other classes might be accused of neglecting their own work, who might be told sharply to "fix your attention on your own work!" assimilate much more than might ordinarily be believed. I attribute this to the obvious fact that they are not under pressure to learn at the higher level. They are urged by just one thing: desire to learn, satisfaction of personal curiosity, if you will.

I do not set a minimum number of words that the boy or

girl must learn at any level. I do make sure that the child knows the words for his reading level. He meets them wherever he turns: on the blackboard, on the news bulletin board, in books above and below his reading level, on flash cards, in class discussions—for their sounds—in projects.

Reading is of first importance. When the retarded child begins his rehabilitation, he starts at the foot of a ladder. He must read on every rung of that ladder. He must read to know the news. He must read to receive letters, must read to write them. He must read to know what signs say, to know where and when to find radio broadcasts. He must read to know anything. He must read to find his way into the vast world of accumulated knowledge, without access to which he *is* a vegetable. If he never learns he remains a vegetable.

Repeat! Repeating has become so habitual with me that I find that I repeat for grown-up listeners and for my daughter, who always grasps the first time whatever is said or read to her.

It is as if the memory of the retarded child were a tablet of stone. The smooth tablet carries no knowledge. Only when words, phrases, are deeply etched on the stone, does the stone retain. Human beings are more flexible than stone, but do not retain as long. Slow learners retain less, and for a briefer period of time, than the so-called "normal"; so more, and more obvious and exacting, etching is indicated.

Even after I have made sure that a child has mastered all the words in a primer, no matter how twisted as to context, I go further. I open the pages of other primers to that child. The stories are written at the same level, but by different writers. They are, then, different stories, new and fresh. As far as the children are concerned, they may have been "promoted," and so they have. Any new word mastered is a personally-acquired promotion. To carry out my first two steps, I make the child "at home" with each new word, as he has become, or is quickly becoming—else he does not learn readily—at home with the class and with me.

When the child recognizes the word, wherever he finds it, he recognizes progress in himself; he has made it. The entire class is made aware—in ways not necessarily subtle—that the child knows those words; so the class also recognizes that child anew, in what he has learned. How valuable is this recognition! Without it the shy, belligerent, aggressive, sullen, slow child will make but painful progress.

I also pay the child in small ways for what he, or she, does. Recognition is payment, and recognition is never withheld. If the child—it is usually, though not always, a girl who yearns for this—feels that only personal contact is recognition enough, she makes the fact known. She comes forward to be patted on the shoulder, or back, or the back of the hand, or to hug and be hugged. None of this personal attention costs me a thing. If I do not bestow it I may set the child back, to poise at the mouth of his burrow, ready to dart back down into his dark inner sanctuary. Boys, of course, are "big and tough." They would not be hugged for anything, except with obvious reluctance! They cringe from the pat on the back or shoulder, hide their faces at the complimentary word, but they never completely evade the caress, or run away from sincere compliments.

I must never promote a child who does not know all he can learn in the grade he is in. If I do, I start him climbing with missing rungs in his ladder of accomplishment. Far too many normal children are promoted regularly from grade to grade, without ever knowing more than a majority—and

I should judge much less than that—of the items they are supposed to master, and retain, in each.

I am not sure that many a junior high school student can read readily at the fifth- or even the fourth-grade level. I am sure he passed, with a satisfactory mark, or he would never have attained junior high, but *did* he pass; if so, how much did he *by*-pass?

I must make sure as far as with me is humanly possible, that none of my children by-pass anything, with reading always and forever the foremost bit of strength in every rung of the ladder of ascent into successful life.

Geography? Arithmetic? Spelling? Drawing?

If the reader really reads, he possesses the sure key to every academic subject, none of which, however, is neglected in favor of reading solely.

V

Ted Threw a Tantrum

I KNEW what was coming when Ted entered the classroom with his mother. So did my class. They knew because, with Ted and his mother, came the principal of the school, and someone else, the custodian. There was one reason why a new pupil arrived with such an entourage. He was a "problem." I knew from experience about how the problem would make itself clear. Ted was almost five feet one inch tall; handsome, sullen, on the defensive.

"I've brought my Teddy to you, Mrs. Smith," began Ted's mother.

"I'm not staying," said Ted. "And don't call me 'Teddy!' I'm no baby!"

"He's *my* baby, anyway, Mrs. Smith," said Ted's mother, "and I've brought him to your class. . . ."

"I'm not going to stay," repeated Ted.

The mother's despairing face became red. I knew in advance that Ted had attended a number of schools. Teachers had thrown up their hands over Ted. Teachers had refused to have anything to do with him. Schools had expelled him.

"Sit down here at my desk, Theodore," I told the big boy.

"I don't like 'Theodore,' either," said Ted. "I like a *manly* name, like Ted."

"Very well, Ted it is," I agreed, granting him a small vic-

26

tory, which he instantly realized, instantly planned to ex-
ploit in some way. For a boy with a low I.Q., I thought, his
mind worked well. That a retarded mind worked so fast
did not surprise me, however. "Sit down at the desk, please."

"No," said Ted, "I'll sit *there!*"

He did pick an empty desk. Sometimes the Teds who
came to me picked desks already occupied, and thus instantly created a problem. I was happy that Ted did not
compound his maneuvering thus. He was attacking, trying
to get his teacher off balance before she could get set.

Ted picked a desk in front of my larger one, where all the
other pupils could see him. I knew, was sure I knew, just
what was coming.

The mother was embarrassed. She did not know whether
to stay and become more embarrassed, or leave and give the
impression of headlong retreat.

"I'll take over," I told Ted's mother. "I do hope you'll
drop in and see what progress Ted makes with us."

"I'll be home as soon as you are," Ted told his mother.

The principal escorted Ted's mother out of the room.

I turned to the class, noting the preliminary signs being
produced by Ted. His lips were a firm line. He was studying the classroom, staring at his new fellow-pupils as if he
were saying:

"Why do you mind this woman, who isn't even your
mother? Watch *me* make her wish she'd never become a
school teacher!"

This was my imagination, of course, for as yet I did not
know enough about Ted to know how his mind worked. I
only knew it was supposed to work slowly, else he wouldn't
be joining this class.

Ted looked around, locating other desks, the cleared space

on the floor, and I smiled inwardly. I had seen this preparation so many times, and found it difficult to blame boys like Ted. What he planned now had always worked.

"Children!" I snapped at the other pupils. It was an agreed-upon signal. They had been staring at Ted with much interest, much curiosity. They wanted to size him up. Now, at my one spoken word, every head was bent over its own desk. Work projects became of prime interest. Books were opened. Faces smoothed out, brows furrowed in concentration.

Ted did a kind of slow roll onto the floor. He hit it hard enough to produce what fiction writers call a "dull thud." But, as other Teds always had in my experience, this Ted did not strike his head, did not hit a desk going down, hit the floor so limply that he could scarcely have been said to fall. It was a practiced, successful production!

Ted began banging his head on the floor, not too hard. Ted began beating a tattoo on the floor with both heels. Ted began moaning as if the death rattle were about to rise in his throat. Ted began moaning and groaning; there is a difference between the two, known to tantrum-throwing children, who do not have to be retarded.

I ignored Ted completely, noting the items I have enumerated above out of the corners of my eyes, and remembering them from experience. I knew so well how the tantrum-throwers began, fell, sprawled, rolled over, rolled back, that I could tell by the sounds, without having to look. To look, I knew, would have been fatal.

My well-schooled children ignored Ted even more completely than I did. They were aware of my methods and how they operated. Three of Ted's predecessors, two of them girls, occupied desks close to Ted's "stage."

I let matters go on a minute or two. One of the girls who had thrown just such a tantrum as this, looked sidewise at me, and would have giggled if I had not placed a warning finger at my lips.

I rose, went to the blackboard. To watch what I did, all the pupils had to turn their backs on Ted. This they did with speed, if with some reluctance.

I wrote the letters "ch" on the board.

"What is that sound?" I asked.

Twelve or thirteen hands shot up. Ted's heels were doing a rhythmic tattoo on the floor. One of my pupils was a comparative newcomer who could not read at all, knew no letters. I wished that one, a girl, to feel herself a part of the class.

"Bette," I said to her, "what kind of a sound does a steam engine make when it is starting?"

"Ch, ch," said Bette, surprised that she had been asked; surprised and proud. She was also a bit uncertain of her answer, but anxious that it be right. Now came that recognition on which all progress with the retarded must be based.

"That's *right,* Bette!" I said, giving her my own recognition of her correct answer. Ted's heels continued their tattoo. Now he was near screaming; screaming would be next. Strange, bloodcurdling, sometimes awesome sounds came from my classroom when newcomers were being "inducted." Now I called upon the class to recognize Bette. "Now that Bette has given you the right sound," I said, "I add some letters to the 'ch' sound, and this is what it becomes." I finished the word "chair."

"Chair!" shouted the class.

I began writing other words beginning with "ch."

"Chop," I wrote.

Ted screamed, but I had timed well. The class, even as Ted screamed, called out the word, some correctly naming it, some not, "Chop." Ted was drowned out, or thought he was. In any event he was markedly ignored. I had taken my place at the blackboard in such a way that, if I snapped a roving glance, I could see Ted's head. As he screamed he raised it, twisted to look at the backs of his schoolmates. Not one paid him any attention whatever!

"Chicken," I wrote. Ted screamed more loudly. The class called out the word "Chicken." Through the thick door of my classroom I am sure the words "chop" and "chicken" were heard in many nearby classrooms, while the screaming of Theodore wasn't heard at all.

"Chest." I wrote. "Chest," yelled the class.

Ted yelled, but his yell was again drowned in the concerted yelling of seventeen members of the class. I joined my voice to theirs to make sure.

I pronounced other words I hurriedly set down, in the event my pupils were slow to rise, or just did not recognize them. In times of stress I sometimes had to pause a bit too long to think of words beginning with "ch."

We kept this up, until a strange, but not at all unusual, event took place.

"Channel," I wrote on the blackboard.

"Channel," came a brand new voice, which rose ahead of all others. It was louder, more resonant. It came from behind the class, over near my desk. Ted had risen and returned to his desk. Ignored as a show-off, he was bound to be noticed.

"Good, Ted!" I gave him full recognition immediately. The word was "channel," after all, rather long for many of my class, especially for the newest, youngest ones.

Instantly the class turned, as one person, and looked at Ted. Then, following my cue, it also gave him that recognition he had failed to attain with banging head, kicking heels, moans, groans, screams. The class applauded.

It was simple. It was effective. Maybe it wasn't dignified, but children are not naturally dignified, and my work is with children; specifically, a rather exceptional kind of children.

"Maybe that was a bit long for some of you," I said to the class, "but it wasn't too long for Ted, was it?"

I seemed to belittle the class somewhat, but the class, as a class, did not mind. It was the individual in the class who was hurt if belittled. I wrote more words. Ted joined with the rest of the class in calling them out. He *might* throw tantrums again, but I doubted it. His first one had been a terrible dud, and he knew it. He was glad of the loophole of escape he had been given.

I returned to my desk, sat down. I ignored Ted for a moment.

When I glanced at him again he had taken the desk I had told him to take in the first place. He appeared to have forgotten that he had thrown a useless tantrum. The class appeared to have forgotten. Nobody had forgotten, really. But everybody had become better acquainted with everybody else in the class, including me.

An hour later the principal poked his head cautiously inside my door. His glance shot to the desk to which I had assigned Ted. Ted was still at that desk. He had not, after all, beaten his mother home.

Not all tantrum-throwers settled for the first ignored tantrum. I once had a boy named Ralph who threw three tantrums before, slow learner that he was, he realized that he attracted no obvious attention. After that he threw no more. Instead, he awaited the arrival of the next tantrum-thrower, so that he could get even by ignoring the "show-off!"

Ted needed recognition. He got it, not for a reprehensible scene, but for something he knew. There was a difference. Maybe he could not have explained the difference, but he knew. Maybe he had not shown me the real key to his inner self, but he and I, and the class, had made a beginning, and would surely find it.

Not one of many tantrum-throwers my class has had in fourteen years has ever been despaired of, transferred to some other teacher, or marked as a failure. One, indeed, an outstanding tantrum-thrower, graduated and became a well-paid supervisor in a contracting business, largely because he would endure no tantrum-throwing on the part of his juniors!

VI

Study the Text

I HAVE found that God does a pretty good job with His world. Experts often shake their heads over Him and His ways, largely because He does not often agree with them. He sends us children we are pleased to call "retarded," to show us, I think, that not everything can be neatly pigeon-holed, channeled, set to music, reduced to a norm; that humanity, especially in its slower manifestations, has no common denominator. The "key" to John will most certainly not fit George's inner door, and vice versa.

The most commonly voiced complaint of educators of the retarded is this:

"There should be books. Where do I find a formula for this work?"

There are books. They are attempts to formula-ize, to fit all boys into a "boy" groove, all girls into a "girl" groove. In the case of those with low I.Q.'s we prefix the word "retarded." It should be, if well thought out, all nice and tidy, if only the retarded boys and girls marched up and conformed. They never do that.

There is only one readable text by which any boy or girl may be rehabilitated: it is the movable text provided by the boy himself, the girl herself. Nothing I can read anywhere can show me the infallible way to the inner self of a child.

33

So what do I do? I face this question every morning when I face my eighteen slow ones. I face it every night, with variations—"what *did* I do; what did I *not* do?"—during my blue hour.

I find no merit in the question of whether religion should be taught in schools; I know one thing, which sets me apart from any part in the religion-in-school controversy: I am unable to reach my children, any one of them, without the Father's help. I recognized this long ago. I have proved it with every "lost sheep." Not a child has passed through my hands without being repeatedly the subject of my heartfelt prayers.

I am not a do-gooder. I am not sanctimonious. I am not saintly. I am just a relentlessly hard worker who is able to work because the Father gives me strength. I am not always telling my children about God in words they will hear elsewhere all their lives. I do not preach, though we do sing songs similar to "Work for the Night Is Coming" and "God of Our Fathers." I am, in this inspiring, awesome task of rehabilitating the retarded, a more or less silent—with respect to religion—helper of the Father.

I look at the faces—some of them would appear rather vacuous if I did not know, or sense, the intelligence behind the apparent vacuity—and ask myself this:

"How can I make God, (the Invisible,) clear to them, when so much they see with their mortal eyes lacks clear meaning to them? How can I make them hear divine music when they can't hear the meaning behind the simplest songs?"

The answer is simple. I do not teach religion. I live it. They can see me. I so live that they wish to emulate me, at least in part, possibly sometimes a very small part where the boys are concerned, a large part with the girls. I do not stand apart, waiting for the Father to manifest Himself in any miraculous way through me. I roll up my sleeves, actually and spiritually, and get busy. I believe that God works closely with every one of His children. Therefore, if I am to be His efficient helper, I must also work closely with each individual.

I pray for help with each child. I don't sit back and await miracles. I don't sit back and say:

"All right, Father, Ted is Yours. Let's see You do something."

Ted was sent to me, in a natural, normal way, because the Father knew I could "find" the boy. In every child I have rehabilitated I have found a segment of myself. With each child I have grown little or much, for which I am most thankful where thanks are due—to the Father. Possibly it is not too much to suggest that this self-finding, for all humanity, is the reason for slow learners, the retarded. The dedicated teacher, without becoming fanatic on the subject, or swerving from the normal in any way, might give the idea a little thought. He will find that it helps approach each new problem which each new slow one poses.

Some wrong things are obvious: (1) people ignore or belittle the slow; (2) people look down on other people from self-assumed heights which may be wholly imaginary, and injuriously so; (3) parents think of themselves, swimming in self-pity, before they think of their "unusual" children as challenges to their mettle; (4) people apologize for the slow learner, and make his path more thorny than it naturally is, by warning others; and those warned, too often heed! (5) Those responsible for the progress of the slow too often shift responsibility elsewhere. (Thus completely refusing the task, the soul-testing, assigned them by the Father.)

I accept my responsibility. I simply make myself available. With His help, without which I am powerless, I succeed with child after child.

There is nothing supernatural about this. Even the atheist does it every day, and he does not believe in God.

I buckle down to the day's business, maintaining that personal, spiritual awareness without which I haven't a chance of reaching any person, especially if that person is slow. By this awareness I read the text of the individual. I am myself slow, since I am *not* God, and so I sometimes stumble over that text for days, even weeks, before I can read it, and know that child, and begin bringing him, or her, into such realization of himself that self-rehabilitation, with all the help I can give him, is certain. By helping a child to help himself, I help children to help one another. I use religion, then, in a practical way. God is not afar off while I am working with His children; He is in the classroom with all of us. He is as real to me as any child. Because this is so, I have no fear that any graduate of my class will lack religious training. He, or she, has it, every minute he, or she, is with me; has it at all other times, too, since if I am to be of most help to any child, I must be memorable to that child, must be taken home in the child's retentiveness, to be on hand and ready for work when the child returns to school next day.

I hope I have made it clear that I regard myself as one of the Father's co-workers, in the evolution of His slower-learning children. He expects of me, for my *own* soul's progress, that though I call on Him for help and guidance, I move as far in every needed direction, on my own steam, as I am humanly able.

Prayer is a simple, practical activity. It is the key which opens the door to task-integration of man with his Maker.

I have a right to go to my principal for answers.

I have a right to go to my supervisor.

I have a right to go to my superintendent of schools.

I have a right to go to my medical, dental, psychological associates.

I have a right to God's help, since he "hired" every last one of us.

Above all I have this right: to realize that the slowest of the slow also have rights I must respect, the world must respect, if it is ever truly to be free.

Where does religion for the child enter here? Naturally enough; it becomes a natural, living thing, along with basic reading, by which each will attain it on his own, because he wants to, and because I have tried to set the right example.

Whether we believe or do not believe in the awareness of God, we must believe in molding the child's character if we are to succeed with him. What good will his ability to read do him, or his ability to make a living, if he has not developed this important phase of his personality? Without it he will shirk responsibility, he will make life unpleasant for those around him, he will place his own selfish needs above the needs of others. He becomes a failure as a citizen and a failure in the search for happiness.

Character building should be a definite part of our daily school work, incorporated into the daily training of our retarded. Most teachers manage to handle this educational task indirectly. The life of many a child has been changed for the best by the interest that some teacher has shown in developing his personality. Indirect molding of character, however, is not enough. We, as teachers and parents, would find many of our headaches removed if we added a specific time for character training every day. To label it the character building period would be impractical. We could call it the social studies program or the citizenship period. To make it successful we would have to make it applicable to the lives of those boys and girls with us at the time. Let me give a practical example. This was a lesson in my own schoolroom with children from eight to eleven years of age. To tell it let me begin with the facts preceding the lesson.

I have two dogs at home. Many of my class visit me from time to time and are acquainted with Fluffy and Duchess, as I call them. Fluffy is a brown and white collie. Duchess is a black cocker spaniel. The collie is rarely on a leash. The cocker spaniel is always on one.

One day at school I read a short story about a dog. Then we began to talk about dogs in general. I finally turned the conversation toward my own two dogs. They asked questions about them and finally one boy asked about the leashes. Why was one dog on the leash all the time and why didn't I keep the other dog tied, too?

"Well," I said, "dogs and people are a great deal alike. Some dogs can be untied because they know how to use their freedom. They do not dig holes, break people's flowers, run away, or go out into the street. They act like well-trained dogs. When taken for a walk they stay with you. When in the yard they play quietly with a toy or take a nap or walk around. Fluffy is that kind of a dog. Unfortunately, poor Duchess is not. She would run away, ruin lawns, or chase automobiles, if she were free. I love her and so for her own good I keep her chained. It makes me unhappy to have to be so harsh with her, but until she learns how to use her freedom she will have to remain tied.

"People are like that, too. Some people steal and they go to jail. Some people are mean to others and find that no one wants to be near them. Other people are happy and kind. They make good fathers and mothers and they have many friends.

"You too are like that. I do not have any favorites in my class. I do allow some of you more liberty than I do others. Just remember Fluffy and Duchess. If you are like Duchess then I always say no when you want to do something. If you are like Fluffy, I give you the chance to use your extra time as you want to use it. All you well-trained boys and girls have to do is the work I have assigned and do it neatly and carefully. After that, like Fluffy, your time is your own because you know how to use that time in the right way."

Did they understand it? Of course they did. You can always tell my second year children from my first. This was a character building lesson. It took a half hour with story and discussion, but it paid dividends in personality development.

VII

Noisy File Cabinets

I GLANCED down the columns of desks right after my class had seated themselves noisily and looked at me as if to ask:

"What do we do today?"

It did not take me nearly as long to think what I am now going to write here as it did to write it. I wanted to see these youngsters as might one who never sees them, as well as the way I always see them. In spite of my dislike of formulae, I found I must work out some form to show what I wished. Let's begin with Carol, since she is the newest girl. Her cold record would read something like this:

Carol B., eight years of age, I.Q. 59, blond, chubby, good appearance, more or less self-reliant. Possibly capable of learning the simplest social adjustments.

I have but to look at the record, even after I have improved it in my mind, to lose faith in many of our institutions. I see in Carol, whose smile is tremulous and warm, though her brows often furrow as if thought were difficult and she wilts as if thinking tired her, the "vegetable" some medical man characterized her. She would, he insisted, only occupy space. She would never go to public school. Her state was hopeless. She would go through a long life or a short one—and the implication was that it would be better for all concerned if it were short—without having more than the foggiest notion that she *lived*. How easily, but for the faith of Carol's mother, that prognosis could have seemed correct. Carol would have been lost. Carol's fault? Not at all. That of some doctor who may, for all I know, have been well-meaning, who set her I.Q. at 47. How many around this country are lost because we try to catalogue people? To mention just one thing about Carol: she reads better than George does, and his I.Q. is 89. Carol will never set the world on fire, but her small bright blaze will be a precious light on this earth to many. Moreover, she will grow up to pay taxes, not to live off taxes paid by others.

Ned R., ten, I.Q. 70, slight blond, underweight, large dark eyes, innately happy disposition, possible rehabilitation.

Of course Ned's rehabilitation is possible. What does the record say? His I.Q. is set at 70. That means that he falls within the general grouping of the retarded. I must find what he does best and develop that ability in such a way as to give him confidence in himself. One thing may handicap his rehabilitation. It has to do with his appearance. I shall write a letter to his mother to tell her to contact me, and at that time we will discuss Ned and his appearance. This will require tact. Ned does not get a haircut as often as he should, possibly because haircuts cost money, even small-boy haircuts, and his parents may not earn much. It does something to Ned when his hair is too long. He seems to feel that it is a banner, shouting in some way to others: "Ned can't get a haircut, he hasn't the money; his people are poor!" What a sweet, serious child is Ned. And how important that child has proved to be. Lost Carol, but for Ned's work as my "teacher's helper," might have remained lost. No, she would not have, but she would have been lost longer, while I hunted the key that Ned found so quickly for me.

Robert G. is ten, I.Q. 63, nearly five feet three, overweight, slouchy, sprawly, pasty complexion, dull of face and of behavior, all reactions slow. He's lazy, uncaring.

I do not have much to add to Robert, not just yet, but he is one of those with whom I labor the hardest, if I can be said to work harder for one than another. Robert seems to hear nothing, see nothing. He sits under rather than at his desk. Sometimes nothing but his eyes move; sometimes only his right hand. He spends the hours, oblivious to all else, looking out the window at the world he, according to the record, will never grasp. What can I do with this boy? I am pondering over him. He responds to little. He does not feel it when I put a hand on his shoulder, just to let him know that there are others around him, others who recognize him. He doodles. He doodles birds, triangles, trees, rectangles, squares. He doodles everything he sees, and he doodles quite accurately. Knowing this, I know what would happen to him in any class save one like mine: he would be taught to use his hands, not his brains.

John J., ten, untidy, I.Q. 58, sullen, incorrigible, rebellious, cruel, brunet, noisy, dull.

I agree with the record that John is ten and brunet. I agree that his established I.Q. is 58. I disagree with almost all else, including that John is noisy. I wish he were noisier, more boy. But of one thing I am sure, as the semester swings into action, he is not dull. Every minute of the day, most days, if I happen to look at him, he seems dull. But he cannot be. I have seen his deep-sunken eyes light up until they were glorious. Why? because of what? I call him Johnny, friendly, congenial, not John, serious, remote, formal. I understand John. I am close to reaching him. If he can create only a slightly larger blaze in the world than Carol, he will have justified himself. My task is to help him to that self-justification. He senses that I can do that, when I call him Johnny.

Peter Y., nine, I.Q. 67, dropped from three schools. Sadistic tendencies. Twists arms. Cruel.

How hideous it looks, the filing case approach to a human being. I cannot accept it, will not. Peter is not to be condemned but helped. I am going to help him. I have noted one thing about Peter which I believe to be *a* key, if not *the* key. He yearns to *be* somebody. He does not want to be on relief like his father. Peter knows he is handicapped, or feels that he is. Both parents have hammered this home to him. Schoolmates have jeered, even as Peter twisted their arms behind them. Girls have screamed "dope, dope, dope" at him, even while he twisted their braids. To him all girls were snarling, spitting cats. But Peter is ambitious, and sadism is his weapon, the vehicle with which he surmounts obstacles. He shall be a member of the school patrol as soon as I can trust him to trust himself. His natural curiosity assures me that eventually he will read well, and do other academic tasks. Peter can be dangerous or economically and spiritually valuable. At this point he may travel either way; it is up to me.

Paul N., thirteen, I. Q. 83, newsboy, counts to ten. Indifferent. Father on relief, regards father as successful. Writes own name, no more; father likewise. Believes himself wise. Prognosis: useless.

I am not going to say too much about Paul here, for a bit later I will write an entire chapter about him. But I will say this: though Paul's I.Q. is 83, I have listened to many boys and girls in average normal classes, who were not his mental equals. Paul has something. He also has, besides a retarded mentality, the feeling that the world owes him a living.

Jane K., ten, I.Q. 60, brunette, overweight, unruffled, goodnatured, continually eating, incurious, without ambition.

Mary L., twelve, I.Q. 89, fearful, hypertense, slackmouthed, tantrums, quarrelsome, rebellious, refuses to learn.

Jeanne A., seven, I.Q. 59, beautiful brunette, aware of it, uneducable.

One comment on Jeanne: she now reads as readily as anyone else in the class.

George Q., twelve, I.Q. 89. Super-extrovert. Already knows more than anybody can teach him. Doesn't read, write, print, unable to count. Loud, quarrelsome.

George is no real problem, sharing the highest I.Q. in the class with Mary L. If he had come to me four years ago, his rehabilitation would have been simple. It still is, though more time will be needed. But just look at the record, without seeing George, and what could you hope for? Your first reaction is that George needs to be taken down a peg. When George came to me the world had been taking him down, peg after peg, for twelve years. But he had fought the world at every peg.

Theodore M., nine, I.Q. 65, blond, five feet one, tantrums.
You have met Ted.

Bette N., seven, I.Q. 51.

What could be more unrevealing than that? Bette, to me, is one of the most beautiful children who ever came to my class. There is a shine about her that even the I.Q. 51 cannot take from her. But so far I know little else about her. I know I can watch her to our mutual profit.

William F., fourteen, I.Q. 88, incorrigible, uneducable, refusing to learn, possibly dangerous.

I agree with the record in just one thing: William F. is fourteen years old, should have come to me six years ago. When he leaves me he will have negated every item in his record.

Philip I., eleven, underdeveloped physically, I.Q. 66, severe introvert, fearful even to speak.

Leave it like that, but for this: Philip loves good, clean clothes, which he wears immaculately.

Edith Z., thirteen, I.Q. 86 completely anti-social.

No! No!

Harriet D., nine, I.Q. 72, nervous, unable to sit still, gossipy, liar, troublemaker, indifferent to learning.

No one is indifferent to learning. The appearance of indifference itself negates the charge, or poses a challenge to the educator. And I do not like to regard myself as an educator; it smacks too much of files, foibles, formulae, routine, hours, schooldays, semesters, I.Q.'s. I am a teacher, yes, but I am also a co-learner, a co-helper, whose task is to help the slow to find that of themselves which only seems to have been left out.

Gudrun C., twelve, I.Q. 80, narcissus.

A brief record indeed, but contains in it—which is unusual with records—an obvious key to Gudrun's rehabilitation.

Naomi E., age fifteen, I.Q. 57. Poor vision, poor hearing, complete personal withdrawal.

Again the key is in the record.

It is almost impossible to translate records into children. Taken from the cold-blooded aspect of case histories in a filing cabinet, it might seem that there is not a promising future for these children. Teachers who make such an assumption cannot hope to do the apparently impossible. We must read within each case history the story of each child at a glance, and detect the possible key that frees that child and starts him toward educational and social adjustment. The key is almost always there, obtainable from the recorded findings of the school psychologist.

VIII

Grist Visitor

I CANNOT pour retarded children into a funnel of formula and catch them normal from the little end. There are many books about the education of the slow learner. I have written one myself. This may be called such a book though that is not my intent. I believe that the best thing to do to escape routine with the retarded is to take, as grist to the mill, everything that comes to hand.

Take visitors. . . .

Some visitors are parents, and these are too close to one child or more to set an example, though whatever happens when a visitor-parent arrives is always discussed after the parent leaves. I never encourage a child to criticize any adult —however much I may feel that the adult merits criticism. I do encourage slow learners to engage in the only criticism I believe to be constructive in any person: self-criticism, or self-analysis.

Visitors to my class are never curiosity seekers; they are always in some way interested. If such a visitor arrives with a chip on his shoulder—the "chip" being a superior attitude, or an over-sympathetic one, or a "down-talking" one—the slowest of my retarded group are instantly aware of the fact. The sensitivity of the retarded child is much greater than even most parents and teachers of the retarded believe.

47

I discourage any visitor I know—if I can find out before-hand—who arrives with the idea of "doing something for the poor dears." My "dears" are not poor, and merit conde-scension from nobody.

Recently an interested visitor entered the classroom un-expectedly. He had visited before, a time or two, and had moved about among the children as if he were one of them. I encouraged this, because if he had sat and talked with me, or spent most of his time sitting beside me, up front, the re-action of the children would have been unfortunate. Men, women, children, all like attention, all yearn for it. No human being can truthfully say that he is indifferent to others' opinions of him, though most people heed conven-tion and hide their urge for recognition, praise perhaps, or open applause, behind an attitude of indifference. The re-tarded child lacks this ability to dissemble. He wishes to be seen as well as to see. If there is a visitor beside me, hands are constantly being raised, boys and/or girls come forward for a closer look, or to show something written, to volunteer to read, to show a drawing, or for some reason that attracts to them the attention of the visitor. The retarded are not different at all in this respect; they simply do not know how to be dishonest about it. They show how they feel, what they desire.

Our masculine visitor had come to look at certain draw-ings. Since he had visited before, the children knew him, smiled at him, made him welcome. Some came forward on their own to shake hands with him; one or two associated him so closely with teacher, whom they hug, that they hugged the visitor also. He regarded such a welcome, nat-urally, as a compliment, and so it was.

I had written a number of simple sentences on the blackboard. There were but two non-readers in the class at the time. All of the class, except Carol, at home with a cold, were present. I told all of the children to put their books in their desks. They did it, noisily. Some were slow. I instructed them to produce their word builders, contained in cardboard boxes. A word builder is a durable piece of cardboard with a capital letter on one side, the lower case letter on the other side. Each box is supposed to contain, to allow for the inevitable misplacements, several small cards of each letter. When I tell the class to piece together, on their desks, the words I have written on the blackboard, they must sort out the proper letters.

"The first one finished *correctly*," I said, "can play his own selection on the phonograph."

There is a phonograph in the classroom, and playing it is considered a treat. I never allow it to be played merely to pass the time. I never do, or allow to be done, anything during class hours, just to pass the time. Minutes a visitor might think are wasted are actually minutes in which I am striving, in every conceivable way, to reach individuals and class.

Two boys and a girl finished the chosen sentence so closely together it was difficult to make sure which had been first. I chose the one I had felt was first.

Instantly the other two objected. They had, they insisted, both been watching the boy I said had won, and both had finished while he was still hunting the last letter. The argument became heated. Heated arguments are common and I do not discourage them, so long as they only approach, but never pass, the point where argument, motion, sound, become disorder. The visitor, even a visiting teacher with experience with the retarded, may think sometimes that my class is unusually noisy, but this is only comparatively so. I learn most about my pupils when their feelings are most deeply touched.

I adhered to my decision, but did not halt the argument. I intended to make use of it after our visitor had left. One unusual thing took place, just prior to the argument. Peter, without permission, quitted his place and moved from desk to desk, helping the slowest learners. They would, in the end, find all the letters—not all the capitals and lower case in the proper places, but there was no chance that any of them could win in spite of their steady prodding. I would have sent Peter back to his desk had I not noted one thing: this lad who had first twisted arms behind backs of boys, twisted braids of girls, *had actually started helping people slower than himself.* His motive may have been to show off for the visitor. His motive may have been anything but that. I chose to believe that he wished to help others. I would find out the proper motive later; for whatever his motive, the result was good. I knew that, when those whom he helped looked at him first with surprise, then with open appreciation.

After our visitor left, I opened a class discussion this way:

"Now, what kind of an impression do you think we made on our visitor, both as a class and as pupils? I'm not going to say. I want *you* to say."

I waited. They were accustomed to new approaches from me. This one was highly experimental. I wished to direct attention to personal behavior.

"It wasn't very nice of us to argue," said John, the untidy boy. "I think he must have thought we were quarrelsome."

I waited for someone else to take it up.

"I don't think teacher made a fair choice," said another. "If she had there wouldn't have been an argument."

"You shouldn't say that, even if you believe it," said a girl, taking my part. "If teacher had given in, to keep the visitor from hearing the argument, we'd try to make her give in all the time, even when we're wrong."

Now that, I thought, was not at all bad for Jane, ten, I.Q. 60. The words may not be exactly hers, since I quote her from memory, but the whole idea is Jane's. Still I waited. The children love discussions like this, if they seem to be going anywhere.

"It wasn't very polite to disagree with the teacher in front of the visitor," said Robert G., ten, 63. One scarcely needs to comment on Robert's perception, even though he was just making use of something he had heard. His words indicated a social awareness I found gratifying.

"Peter," said Naomi E., fifteen, I.Q. 57, whose natural policy was always one of complete withdrawal, "showed off too much. He knew he could find letters faster than others, and he wanted to make sure our visitor knew he was faster!"

That was not only surprising, interesting, but highly devastating. Peter had become actively and loudly irritated over much less. The class knew it, went silent, looked at Peter to see how he would take it. Peter·was staring at Naomi, his own complete opposite.

"You're right," said Peter simply, "and I wish I could be sorry I do things like that. Even if I can't be sorry, I wish I could hold myself in!"

And how did the class take Peter's humility, his strange regret? The class broke into applause, and only Peter seemed not to know why.

When the discussion ended I had but one regret: that our visitor had not stayed to hear every word of it. But then, he already knew that so-called retarded minds were good minds; good, but slow; and maybe not nearly as slow as average normal people might take for granted.

IX

Keys in Small Corners

MANY educators hold that the retarded child can be taught to use his hands, but little else. I am sure that any child able to work with his hands can use his brain. He can also be taught to read. The child who does not read loses most of the value of our modern world. It is criminal to train hands at the expense of brains. It is criminal, just because the teaching calls for care, understanding, love, and application, *not* to teach the child to read, even if he remains in primers for for a year or two beyond the average. Words are keys to living.

An illiterate child within reach of any school, who has attended school, is inexcusable, and who ever is responsible merits utter condemnation. Most children above an I.Q. of 50 can learn to read. It requires work, dedicated work, than which there is nothing more rewarding.

In my class the emphasis is placed on academics. I also teach some carpentering, sewing, and weaving, but I teach these in an art period four times a week. Manual art does not become the main objective in my class. It has a certain therapeutic value, I believe, but I give it in small quantities for good academic work or for good effort. Since we use mostly scrap materials my complete lumber bill is less than $12 a year. My sewing and weaving materials average less than $10. The only other special materials I require are Shaw finger paint, Shaw Finger Paint paper, bookbinding tape, and cardboard. Even for the latter we are usually able to get old posters used by the junior and senior high. I use these last items for making project and library books with material original with the class and myself. The art supplies given to the regular classes are also supplied to my class. Thus my special needs cover about $25 a year. Here the big expense of special class work is eliminated and the emphasis is placed first on mental, physical, and social rehabilitation, second on academic work, then on crafts. Almost nothing, in the way of equipment, can be found in my classroom that cannot be found in a normal classroom at the same levels. (Remember, however, that I now teach children under eleven.) I cannot teach pupils not to waste taxpayers' money by wasting it myself. My techniques have, definitely, their practical commercial side. I want my pupils, every one, to make their own way, never to be indigent.

The program begins with reading. I cannot repeat that too often. For reading is the master key—to other academic subjects, and to life. By speech we communicate with a restricted few, with one another, in a small orbit. By reading we reach the world.

The class draws things, with colored crayons. I provide the paper. It is not expensive paper. It costs no more than paper used in normal classes.

Most teachers encourage pupils to cover each sheet with whatever they draw. I do not. I reserve a small corner for my own use. That corner is the key by which I hope to open the door of the small artist. It is also the key, and the key-

hole, by which the artist opens the door of the world to efficient living at whatever his level may prove to be.

Let's take Bette N., seven, I.Q. 51; William F., fourteen,
I.Q. 88; Harriet D., nine, I.Q. 72; Gudrun C., twelve, I.Q.
80. Do not try to remember those cold records; just remember the only importance, the children themselves.

Bette is new, an unknown quantity, I.Q. just high enough
to send her to public school, and to my class. She is a non-
reader. But like every child she enjoys working with colored
crayons. She draws things. Their roughness is natural, but
she strives to make them look like things she has noticed.
Before she begins, I call Bette to me. With two lines I cut
off a corner of the sheet on which she will draw. In it I
print the word which I intend to be all-important, for the
time being, to Bette; the word is "Bette." I print it slowly,
carefully.

"This is your name, darling," I tell her. "See how I draw
it? It has five letters, the same number of fingers and thumb
you have on one hand. Spell it after me: B . . . e . . . t . . .
t . . . e."

Sometimes Bette, conscious of her lacks, does not try to
follow me. Usually, she does.

"We'll try to remember what it looks like, won't we,
Bette?" I ask her.

"Yes," says Bette.

"Now don't run any color into this square I've made. See
this shape? The two lines I drew, and the two edges of the
paper. They form a square. You draw in all the rest of the
sheet, but not in the square. You leave that, so when your
drawing is pinned on the wall, where everybody can see it,
everybody will know that Bette drew it."

"If they can *read,* they can," amends Bette. "I can't. I can't read."

"But what did I tell you these five letters were?"

"My name, Bette!"

"There, you see? You can almost read right now. Soon you'll be able to."

A simple beginning, as anyone can see, but not for the retarded child. It is a monumental problem sometimes, to find a beginning. One thing Bette does, I notice, after she has filled the rest of her sheet with smears of color—combined smears which may or may not have the shape Bette insists— she disobeys me, in a way. She does not extend her colors into the square I made, no. She pencils something in. With tongue outthrust in token of concentration, she tries to draw the letters of her name, as nearly as possible as I drew them. The key I have found may not be an exact fit, but it will open at least the outer door.

Moreover, when Bette's drawing is pinned on the wall, Bette herself can find it. Her classmates look over the drawings, and she hears them murmur her name. She beams and is proud; she would beam and be proud if her I.Q. were 42, or even lower, though how much lower I fear to say.

I reserve a corner for myself on William's sheet, in which I write: "See the boy. He is on the wall. His name is William."

Now, William knows his own name when he sees it. In fact he can read a little; he can read what I have written on his sheet. It is important that I do not forget that. William is a kind of savage. I am going to use his incorrigibility for his rehabilitation. In every way I play on that theme.

"Now, William," I say, "draw a boy. He is on top of a wall, high above everybody else. His name is William. William, you can see, likes to be above everybody else, so he can look down on them. And, William, if you do a good job, a good *enough* job, your drawing will be pinned on the wall where everybody will *know* you've done a good job."

"What colors do I use?" asks William, much interested, because this job has been given a personal touch. William makes a concession, asking me what colors to use. If I volunteered and told him first, he would rebel, possibly argue; even if he does not believe inside him that he knows best, he assumes the attitude.

"Use your own good judgment, William," I say. "Your drawing should look like a boy, the wall like a wall, and William . . .

"Like me?" grins William,

"You can try hard, anyway!"

How utterly simple it appears, when seen thus, in print; but in actual practice it is not simple. The teacher must find her own way into the spirit of each child. If she does not find the key she loses the child, or the child, already lost, is never found.

Every child has an assignment. I talk briefly with each child before drawing starts. Then I print a few words which tell a simple story, a different story for each child, more complicated for the more advanced, tell each child to leave my corner open. Then, the children simply illustrate what I have written.

Where this is not done, in drawing alone, few slow children are imaginative or inventive. They copy. No special thought, save in the mixing or use of crayons, and composition, enters into the drawing.

When I print something, however, the child must think, ever so little, to make his drawing fit what I have printed.

And there, all during the drawing, he sees what I have printed. Seeing words makes words the seer's own, given time and opportunity. Eventually I change from printing to script, as the child learns.

In a week I make sure that every child has seen every letter in the alphabet, both capitals and small letters. I make sure that words found in primers and readers appear in the corners I have reserved for myself.

The space above my blackboards is filled with drawings. Every child is eager, even William, to see his work up there, where everybody else can see it. He strives to make sure it reaches such eminence.

Bette masters her name and its five letters.

William discovers, to some extent, that it is a good thing to stand high on a wall, if he has reached it by his own efforts—by a good drawing, let us say—and is subtly urged to better his next drawing.

I do not lose those drawings. I leave them on the wall, however, only until I am sure that every pupil has done better, has made progress, both in drawing and reading, in printing or writing. I collect each pupil's drawing, as soon as there is another to compare with it, and study both carefully for evidence of progress. Not even the pupil himself, or herself, is more heartwarmingly delighted than I am when progress is clearly shown.

Then, each pupil and I study that pupil's work, and share our discovery that he or she has made progress. I do not need to be shown that I, too, have made progress.

Not all of the keys are drawings.

I write sentences on the blackboard. I transfer them to bulletin boards. I require pupils to copy them. The best copyists find their work also pinned to the space above the blackboard.

Nothing pleases children more than for other children to take note of drawings and printings or writings, and when visitors show interest . . . !

There are many ways in which, socially, children can show their adequacy. Whenever one shows progress in any direction, even one that has never been a matter of record, the fact is written on the blackboard for all to see, like this:

FOR GOOD MANNERS

Gudrun****

Bette**

William*

Human beings reach for the stars, even small stars on the blackboard in an obscure public school. Having attained one star, human beings yearn for others. Slow learners are the most human of human beings.

My keys, I realize, are but glimpses. But if, in the course of this writing, I give you enough glimpses, like the phonograph records in the next chapter, for example, you begin to get a fairly complete picture. If you are interested, as a parent, teacher, or observer, in slow learners, my glimpses will give you a glimmer of a complete picture. Bear in mind that one picture is only remotely like another, especially if the images are slow children, every one of whom must be reached as an individual.

The task is fascinating. It is rewarding.

It is dedicated ministry.

It is "family" in a way that too few blood-relative families appreciate. They must be inspired to appreciate it if we are to rehabilitate more small slow ones, before they become big, lumbering, indigent slow ones.

X

For the Records

ALERTNESS is necessary, for the retarded themselves are alert. If they are alert to snubs and slights, one loses them. If they are alert to progress—which few will be by themselves—they prove themselves. They emerge slowly, cautiously, but they emerge. They never cease to surprise, and sometimes startle, me. They always interest me.

Edith Z., "thirteen, I.Q. 86, completely anti-social," departed from character. Sooner or later every slow child does. Each one of them awaits the opportunity to depart. Watch and wait for the departure, and catch your "lamb." Or the "lamb," with encouragement and understanding, catches itself.

Edith, who did not like anybody and did not want anybody to like her—she said so if given an opportunity—brought me a number of victrola records.

"Might as well bring 'em here," said Edith, "as throw them out with the trash!"

She was trying to say that bringing the records to the class was the same as throwing them in the trash. One might think that sort of comment a large bit of cerebration for a retarded child, but I have found that even the severely retarded sometimes make comments that would make a genius' mouth fall slackly open. A genius, by the way, will

often make comments that make the retarded regard him as
a "dope."

I studied Edith as she compared the schoolroom into
which she had been inducted to "trash."

"Do you really think that, Edith?" I asked softly.

She tossed her head. "I do," she said. But I did not hear
the words, not really. I saw the tears at the corners of her
eyes. There was some other reason why she had brought the
records.

"What am I to do with them?" I asked. She must have
had some idea, else she would not have brought them.

"I heard the kids say they wished the old Victrola here
worked, or that there were some new records."

"But you don't *care* what the kids say!"

"No!" she said explosively. "But there are words on the
records; maybe the kids ought to learn them."

I would have thought of that—maybe. And it was a good
idea. Some of the words of the titles were longer than even
the most advanced of my pupils knew. But they were
known titles. Possibly the children had heard the titles on
radio, television, other media of popular music. My pupils
could piece titles together and guess—then confirm what
the long words were.

I took the records to a desk near the blackboard. I ran
through the records in order, setting down their titles clearly
on the board. Behind me the class was silent. I carried the
records to my desk and then deliberately disarranged their
order, so that it would not be the same as it was on the
blackboard. I spoke to the class.

"Edith," I said, "has brought something very useful. Records we can play on our Victrola—if the Victrola works."

"It works," said Peter. "I fixed it yesterday."

Nobody heard him except myself. The class was studying Edith with new interest. Never before had she offered to do anything for anybody, or seemed to care what I felt about her—what anybody felt about her. After a long thoughtful moment—and moments can become almost painfully thoughtful with the slow—the class applauded. Edith, the "anti-social" one, was close to tears. She was proudly embarrassed by unaccustomed attention.

"We're going to use the records in our studies," I told the class. "First, I'm going to allow some one of you, the first one who believes he can read the titles, to go to the board, indicate a title, read it to the class. Then, he'll go to my desk, find the record of that title, take it to the Victrola and play it. While it is being played, the rest of you will work out the title, on your desk, with your word builders. The first to finish gets to select the next title to be played, and will play it when he has found the record among the records on my desk. If no one finishes the title with the word builders, the boy or girl who is playing the first title plays it again."

That was a rather lengthy bit of instruction, but the class grasped it. One thing I would like to make clear. I never talk down to any child. And I always talk to the chronological age of the individual—as an individual, not as a member of the class—rather than to his mental age. He may not completely understand me when I talk to his chronological age, but he understands enough to make an accurate guess; and he always knows, and always resents, if he is "talked down" to.

"Since Edith brought the records," I went on, before she could cringe from her new responsibility, "she will correct anyone who doesn't read the titles correctly. And, if asked, she will help find the corresponding titles among the records she brought to us."

Edith was much pleased. More and more she was being withdrawn from her withdrawal from society, as represented by her schoolmates. And she was enjoying it. It made her blush, and show tears, but a happy blush, and pleased tears.

She smiled tremulously, ready and eager to assume her temporary responsibility toward her fellow pupils.

Peter was eager to start. He always insisted on being first. William—one never could be sure about William. All faces were eager as lips moved to spell out titles. Hands shot forward, fingers snapped for attention. They knew I disregarded the finger-snappers. One boy almost turned his back, the back of his head held in his palm, his elbow slouched on his desk. Paul, the untidy.

Paul hated, or affected to hate, the word builders. He felt he could read without them.

"Paul," I said, "suppose you make the first choice."

He whirled, his face a mask of outrage. He had not asked to be considered in this new technique of words. I could see his mind work. He was about to call out: "I didn't hold up my hand!" when it occurred to him that the other pupils might think he was somehow afraid. Then the second idea came to him. If he played the Victrola while the others built words, he would not have to build words himself.

Paul went proudly to the blackboard. What if he did not read the title of his choice correctly? There was Edith to correct him; he would not be corrected by the teacher, in front of everybody.

He made his selection. He read it correctly. Edith did not correct him. Nor did I. Nobody did. Paul was amazed—and delighted. He almost ran to my desk. He worked through the pile of records, glancing at the titles. I offered no help. He did not call on Edith. I held my breath. If he picked the wrong record—and there were more wrong than right ones —most of the class would know it when the Victrola started playing. If they laughed at him . . .

But Paul could endure laughter, though not from me, or any adult—or any pupil from any other room where mysteriously superior boys and girls were found.

Other pupils scarcely gave a thought to the matter. They were busy with their word builders, each trying to be first. The first to finish would turn to me and hold up his hand, her hand.

The Victrola began playing. Paul had picked the correct title.

The music swelled in the classroom. Paul walked to me and said:

"You, see? I did it right. I don't *need* those silly old word builders."

"Maybe not," I partially agreed with him, "but several of the others *do* need them. Why don't you, while the music plays, go help some of the others to spell out the title of your favorite piece of music?"

Paul grinned.

"Most of them," he said, "already *have* help!"

It was true. Edith and Peter had both finished their word-building job. Neither had held up a hand. Edith, of course, did not particularly care to choose titles she was discarding from her home, but Peter . . .

Peter was deliberately vacating his right to be first—after Paul. Peter, the sadist, was showing new facets of character, giving others a chance—as he had given none a chance when he had first come to class.

Bette, of course, could not do much of anything with the word builder. Peter squeezed into the seat with her, became her "teacher." Bette looked up at him, wide-eyed—as she had probably never before looked at any one, adult or child. She beamed. Peter affected not to notice, but his awareness was as transparent as cellophane.

Records—of a kind—had their uses after all.

XI

Symbol of the Stairs

MY CLASSROOM is on the third floor. The gymnasium is in the basement. Even "Mrs. Smith's Class" has a gym period. It is not long, for slow attentions are not firmly held. Just outside my door, and to the right along a rather gloomy hall, opposite my door, is the balcony of the auditorium. One enters the balcony from its top and looks down two floors to the stage. By a trick of vision the stage seems to lean forward, and to be closer to the balcony than it is. One must see it from below for proper perspective. The auditorium, or theater, is an awesome place when there is no one in any of the seats. I have often sat alone in the darkened balcony, listening to the whispers. And often I have encountered one or more of my pupils there, separated from each other by many seats; I wondered what their imaginations heard among the whispers.

Most of them find it easy to move into the balcony and just sit with dreams. Some of them like to sit behind the classroom windows and look out at the laundered skies, or the mares' tails of storm, or the leaves of autumn.

I have often wondered if they comprehend the symbolism I have found here, and have found so useful.

Take gym period. . . .

I can conduct my small class down to the gym. At first I

do that. We traverse the hall, with the yawning black pit of the theater on our left, the two entrances like mouths with the upper lips bitten off. Our small feet—I am not very big myself—beat out a timid tattoo on the tiles. The feet of the normal strike the floor with tremendous confidence; their owners have no fear of others' glances and frowns. They know themselves, in their fearless world—or think they do, which amounts to the same thing—and that is what I wish for my slow ones to think. There are three flights of stairs. There are seldom lights on in the basement. Save for the lights we turn on in the gym, the basement is dark—as dark as the world of the unrehabilitated slow. My imagination can picture the darkness as teeming with terrors; I can fancy what the retarded may see in the shadows.

It is from just such shadows most of them have fled even before, at their youngest, they come to me.

I begin at once to choose from among them, boys or girls who show something of leadership. I seldom find either a boy or girl who is not eager to lead. And the eager to lead can be led, or taught to lead themselves.

"I want some boy who is sure he can form the class in column, keep them in column, and take them down to the gym while I just watch. I want that boy to decide what game is to be played, and be able to tell the others how to play it. Who'd like to try?"

They often surprise me. The slowest, the seemingly slowest, show self-confidence. I am aware, though, that if all the class save the volunteer were normal, this boy or girl would not volunteer. He has no fear of leading his own level of intelligence. And that, for me, is good enough. My job is to raise the level at which he feels confidence.

And while I am finding boys and girls ready to lead, I am

finding something else: boys and girls capable of serving on the school patrol, which signals children across the streets at dangerous corners.

"You'll all get a chance," I tell the class. "If you're not chosen now, or are timid about trying now, you'll be chosen later, or will feel better about trying after you've watched a bit how it goes."

They all look interested.

"And every one of you has a chance to be a member of the school patrol, and wear one of those white belts with the broad white strap across your front and back. You know how nice it looks."

If this looks like shameless catering to vanity, so be it. It works. It works with everybody.

The first time I send my column of tall and short boys and girls, stumpy and fat boys and girls, sleek and untidy boys and girls, away from the classroom in an organized group, out and down through the yawning abyss of the cavern which is the school, with a new leader, I am a little afraid. But all I have to say to myself is, "O, ye of little faith," and I know it will be all right. Just the same, I feel that way until they have more practice. I follow along after, giving them time to get out of sight, and enter the gym after they have taken their places. It is always a great relief to find them all accounted for, all having a good time.

And they do have a good time. Usually what they enjoy most is throwing the basketball around. They have all seen big fast normal boys and girls make baskets. To make baskets is a symbol of normalcy. So now the leader picks out a boy or girl, sets him or her apart from the others.

"Catch the ball when I throw it. Then throw it into the basket."

He does not add, "if you can." He takes it for granted that the player can, as he hopes it will be taken, in his turn, that *he* can. He throws the ball high in the middle of the circle of players. The designated child runs forward and catches the ball. If he does not catch it, the next designated tries. When one catches the ball, he tries for the basket. And when a basket is made the sounds from the serious-faced others is loud, enthusiastic, and prolonged. A listener, not in the gym, would think that a regular game was in progress, and that someone had worked a miracle of point-making. And someone has. And everybody else is pleased.

When I first take my class to the gym I try to make sure that every child makes a basket before returning to the class-room. There should be no failures, even such small ones, for children who expect to fail. And when they have suc-ceeded a few times they expect to succeed and therein is victory found.

They do not run around much in the gym. They are boys and girls, and boys can get rough without realizing it. And there is something else: as minds of the retarded are not as lively as those of the normal, so the bodies are not as lively, and it is not at all unusual, early in any game, especially if he or she has failed to make a basket, for one of the group to come to me, or to the leader, and say:

"I don't feel like playing. I'm tired."

I do not argue. The leader is told not to argue. I instantly agree that the player may sit down. I never apply pressure. Invariably, after a brief rest, the player returns of his own accord. What he thinks, I do not know. I only guess. Results count, and we do get results.

In order that my gym formation interfere as little as pos-sible with other activities of the school—a school so large that many boys and girls are almost always moving swiftly up or down the stairs—formation in column is maintained. To keep the children from stepping out of line, the leader calls out to boy or girl who does—usually trying to take a shortcut on a stair landing. The children are obedient to their own. Each expects to be leader one day; each expects others, in his turn, to obey him.

Very early in a new semester I find it unnecessary to lead my class down to the gym. They find their way accurately, swiftly, confidently, right down to the basement, where they conduct their periods themselves. Bells often ring for various reasons throughout the school, so my class knows which bells mean it is time to return to the classroom. They seldom make mistakes. Too many of them are eager to get back to their somewhat noisy studies. They all enjoy the importance, too, of remaining in formation just outside the door, while some, with verbal permission from the leader—who is in charge until he has returned them all to their seats—drop out to drink at the fountain behind the yawning pit of the theater.

My pupils soon learn all the ways about the school building they need to know. They become confident that they know just where to go, alone or with others. They delight in showing visitors around.

From the schoolroom to the school building, they enlarge their small horizons. Mothers sometimes bring their children who, having learned the school building, learn the school yard, then adjacent streets, then the way to and from their homes. When all have proved themselves capable of traveling, singly or in groups, between their homes and school, they have accomplished much.

The stairs as a symbol becomes clear. The first step is to

help the child to find his way out of his own fearful darkness, into which the ignorant scorn of his fellows has sent him scurrying.

The last step, of course, is the world outside school. But when the children have mastered—really mastered, not slipped and slid over—all the stairs, real and symbolic, which I have mentioned here, I have little fear of the outside world for them, and they have little fear for themselves.

Not just the stairs, not just records, not just drawing with corners bearing my printing, not just blackboards, bulletin boards, handcraft, constitute the simple tools of rehabilitation, but all of them together, and all new ones that come to hand. There are sometimes enough, but there are never too many.

Nothing delights me as much as this kind of a remark from a visitor, and some variation of it is often made:

"But I can't tell the difference between these children and *normal* ones. How do *you* tell?"

Alas, there are ways to tell. There are, in fact, so many ways to tell that there are far too many ways in which the wisest of us can be dead wrong about the so-called "retarded" children.

There are always stairs the retarded find difficult; stairs up and down which the normal jump, slide, or run with thoughtless self-confidence. That, in the outside world, the normal sometimes find themselves on the payrolls of my erstwhile pupils does not alter the simple fact that the stairs can be difficult and discouraging.

XII

Superiors Make or Break

WHILE I devote a special blue hour to my pupils, I devote many thankful hours to consideration of my superiors. A principal, I know from experience, can build or destroy by as little as a single word. Once, long ago, a principal told me this:

"You're with me because I can't help myself. I don't believe in special education. I think it is a waste of time."

I would like to be able to say that eventually I won him around to a feeling for the retarded ones who could not, as he believed, keep up with normal children if enough pressure were placed on them. I am able to say only that he found it possible to educate them, as the yearly tests proved. He never did like them in his school. I did not argue with him. That is bad public relations. I never argue with my superiors for myself or my ideas. I set out to prove to this particular principal that special education was an oasis in the deserts of the world to the shy, withdrawn, retarded child. I let him see for himself. The idea always remained distasteful to him. My children never lost their feeling of inferiority in that school.

For some years I have been blessed with principals who either have had an earnest desire to help every child in the school or have known the problems confronting the teacher

72

of the retarded. The latter have been men who have themselves taught the retarded. Without understanding teachers, and principals who understand their problems and their pupils, the retarded are lost indeed. This is true, of course, of the so-called normal child, for all his greater inclination to fight for himself. It is more than true of the retarded child who sees all the world of people as different from himself.

I began to see my role differently after my principals and other superiors showed me to myself, not only as they saw me, but as the pupils and their parents were bound to see me. I was not a savior of the world; I was a servant of the slow of the world, and the slow might one day save the world. Certainly they would be saved *to* the world if I, and teachers like me, properly understood their roles.

Some progressive educators have already taken the stand that teachers of special education will soon become, in effect, public relations officials and counselors—which requires some explanation. Teachers of normal classes, though closely associated with their pupils, are not nearly as closely associated as are teachers of special classes, where the contact is personal for each and every child separately. And what I say to Carol, or George, or Sam, or Janet, and what I do to them, or with them, becomes of vital importance, not just to the pupils and me, but to my school and my community. Children have a way of picking examples to follow. The retarded are even more prone to do this than the normal, for they are closer, so close that they often regard their teachers as aunts, mothers, grandmothers, cousins, nieces—people who have been good to them, have understood them. And these children, who seek good examples, *must find them in their teachers*.

I cannot expect my girls to keep their hair combed if I do not.

I cannot expect my boys and girls to dress neatly if I do not.

I cannot expect my boys and girls to write well, or read clearly, or print, or walk, or do anything properly, if I do not.

I cannot expect my pupils to be truthful if I equivocate; and the retarded question falsehood as fast as do the normal, and find less excuse for it, even in their examples.

I cannot expect abstemiousness in my pupils if I am greedy.

I cannot expect courtesy in my pupils if I lack courtesy.

I cannot expect my pupils to be pleasant if I am shrewish, or lack consideration for others, any others.

I may make mistakes, and prove myself human, as my pupils are, but I must not cover my mistakes with evasions; I must admit them, caution my pupils not to make the same errors, and try myself never again to make them.

Neatness, like beauty, to which it is closely akin, is more than skin-deep; it is heart-and-soul deep; it is spirit deep. If I am only outwardly neat, my pupils become aware quickly, in strange intuitive ways, that underneath I am slovenly. Therefore my outward neatness must be sincere, and all the way in, or my pupils will know. Why? Because, possibly, *I* know, and knowledge makes me give myself away. I explain neatness to my small ones, citing examples, from picking up after themselves at school and at home, to brushing behind their teeth, where nobody except the visiting dentist at school ever looks.

Once a retarded child begins to comprehend my objectives with him, he must have faith that, with me, he will obtain those objectives—the principal of which is to fit him for some useful niche in society.

It is clear, then, where I am a public relations official. It is clear that the measure of my success is what my pupils say of me at home, among their friends, and what their parents say of me to their friends. I must, though it be called "politics" by the non-understanding, make sure that what is said of me is good. If it is not, my school also suffers.

How am I a counselor?

This is part and parcel of the public relations task. Whatever I say to a retarded child that serves to advance him, even infinitesimally, is counseling. I do not have to be a psychiatrist to know this, nor a psychologist, though it may help a great deal if I am both. But if I am not, my knowledge of people, my experience with children, must serve me in lieu of formal knowledge of psychiatry and psychology.

I have said that parents are always welcome in class. When they come they often ask me questions.

"Why won't George pick up his clothes at *home*; he does it here, for *you*?"

I must have an answer for the mother who asks me this kind of question. While I may serve as an example to a pupil, I am not an example to parents, nor should I ever take the stand that I am. I do not tell a mother that if she behaves toward her child as I do, he will consider her as he considers me. No. For I am not the child's mother, she is not the child's teacher *per se*. I try to tell her what I would do *if* I were the mother. Happily I have a little experience in this, because I am a mother, though not of a retarded child.

How different is a retarded child, really, from a normal child? Much less than is generally believed except by progressive educators, among whom my principals for some years now have been numbered. Not only have they, and their closer staff members, grasped the significance of special education, but they have taken care of the greatest task of all: integration of the retarded child into the school system as a child, not as a different child. They have been opposed to segregation in name, attitude, and fact.

It is almost unheard of in my school for a teacher to make this kind of remark:

"John, if you don't learn your lessons better, I'll send you to join those dumbells in Mrs. Smith's class."

I have known teachers who have lacked understanding of the retarded child, have regarded him instead as rebellious, stubborn, mean. They have held our classes over the heads of rebellious or slow normal children in exactly the fashion indicated.

A remark like that above, on which many variations are possible, can destroy the work of the special teacher because it starts normal children taking note of "differences," inspires them to snobbishness, to adopt superior attitudes. It never happens in my school, and I pray that it does not happen where any other special educators have their peculiarly personal problems. The finger of the normal child and adult is too often pointed at the slow child outside the school.

Now I must use a word of caution here. No teacher, no principal should ever integrate the retarded child into a school in this fashion:

"William is different, doesn't learn very fast, and he is sensitive about it, so you must pay no attention to him. Treat him as you would a normal child. Pretend you see no difference in him!"

Nobody can spot this kind of evasion quicker than the retarded child, for it is a peculiarity of his slowness that he is fast to spot insincerity. Even if he can not name it, has no words for it, he senses it, withdraws from it, and so negates the best efforts of teacher and principal. My principals have understood this better than I have. They themselves treat their pupils, normal and retarded, as nearly alike as individuals themselves will permit; they require the same consideration from all members of their staffs.

Occasionally I have reasons to leave my class unexpectedly. When occasion demands, my principal, having himself taught the retarded, can, and willingly does, step into my shoes as if he belonged in them. The children, knowing, accept him as they accept me. Of course they may try to show off a little, for they know as well as I do that he is the principal, the superior not only of the pupils themselves but of their superiors, their teachers.

I need scarcely point out that when the principal who knows, substitutes for the special teacher, if for only an hour or so, that teacher has not served herself well in the public relations department, or as a counselor, if the principal can, without half trying, pick flaws in the discipline, deportment, or academic ability of the special class.

If a teacher of a special class has any reason to fear the principal as her own substitute, then she must realize that she has not done her complete task. If, knowing his knowledge of the retarded, she feels the need of covering up, it is because she has, and knows it, shortcomings to hide from his experience.

I welcome the chance to substitute my principal for myself. I must always be able to say this to myself. If, however, he is hostile to special education—why, then I have a rather special problem personally .

I am most thankful that I do not currently have this problem. I shall be happier, day by day, to learn that, here and there, superiors of other teachers come to a better under-standing of the rich rewards, to teachers as well as pupils, of special education. Rich rewards? I do not even think of financial rewards for teachers, whose richest rewards will, doubtless, always be spiritual. I do sometimes think of finan-cial rewards for my pupils, many of whom have been suc-cessful in their niches in the business world. A comfortable number of graduates have returned of their own free will to thank me for my help in making this possible.

This, too, is good public relations, for everybody con-cerned.

It is the ultimate in counseling.

XIII

Small Hours of Gold

My BLUE hours are for my current retarded children. My golden hours are for those who have graduated from my class but return at unexpected moments to talk with me. More do this than I expect, and often the boys and girls I least expect return to me, and usually all the day, the hour, the classroom, is brighter. If a graduate is ashamed to return, then I have sent him forth only half taught. If he does not realize that he has found himself in my class, then he has not, and I have failed.

Just today Roger came in, and the instant I saw him I drew my tender shins under my desk. I remembered. I had excellent cause never to forget. For besides being retarded, Roger was big and awkward. If he accidentally brushed against a girl in his class, he sent her spinning—and, likely enough, screaming. He was always big for his chronological age, bigger still for his mental age. He was an affectionate boy. He would pat my shoulder, and my shoulder would be bruised.

Before Roger first came to me, a man teacher had delivered an ultimatum to his principal:

"Either Roger goes or I do! I won't go a step further with that hulking boy."

It was inevitable that Roger learn early that his size had

a subduing effect on all children, and was regarded with something akin to awe by adults. Fortunately he was, for the most part, good-natured. He was also mischievous. The teacher who delivered the ultimatum regarding Roger— well, Roger had set out to best that teacher in every way of which a "slow, retarded" child could think. He organized pupil revolts against the teacher. He made strange sounds in his throat and was all innocence when charged with making them; but other children knew, and laughed, uncontrollably. There was no discipline.

Roger came to me, and after I had studied him awhile— after we, together, had studied Roger—I simply used his help with other children. I gave him recognition and responsibility. I helped him to make something of himself. I wish I might add that he thereafter behaved with every other adult as he did with me, but that would not be true. I had reasons for leaving the class, sickness perhaps, and substitutes were found. My current principal, needless to say, was never one of those substitutes; this was before his time.

Roger made life miserable for every substitute. He told me frankly that he was going to make it impossible for me to leave the class—and Roger himself. Each substitute delivered an ultimatum after one experience:

"I'll never teach that class while that boy Roger is in it!"

Roger even told another teacher:

"I'm right back in the groove with all substitutes, just as I was when I made that last teacher yell 'Uncle!'"

One substitute, when I was ill, wanted to throw in the sponge at noon, and only with difficulty was induced to teach an entire day. But I had little trouble—save with Roger's size and awkwardness.

The instant Roger entered, to grin down at me from his

superior height and bulk, I remembered the last time he had sat down at the desk with me, and had accidentally kicked me on the ankle with his huge, hard shoes. He almost fractured my ankle. He did not mean to, of course, but it hurt no less because his intentions were of the best. And I did not dare tell him how he had hurt me, or he would have, probably, sought to comfort me—and harmed me even more.

Roger was the proverbial bull in the china shop; he broke all the china, wherever he went. But he did manage to read adequately, and learn enough mathematics and other subjects to hold his own with average normal people in the world of adults.

Now, he had returned to tell me so. He stopped just inside the door. Possibly he, too, remembered, and was taking no chances. There were many items in the classroom, as he well knew, which he could break without even trying.

"I just came back to see you, Miz Smith," said Roger.

"I'm glad to see you, Roger—I think!" I said, though I said the last two words to myself.

We shook hands, somewhat diffidently on my part, for my small hand was lost in his large one. But this time he was gentle.

"I just came back to thank you," he said. "I have a good job. I have had a good job ever since I graduated. I owe my ability to handle it to you, and I just thought you'd like to know that."

"I *do* like to know it," I said. "I think it's fine of you to return and tell me. It will help me a great deal to do well by today's pupils."

"That's what I thought," said Roger. "I gave you a lot of trouble, though, and I'm sorry. I hope you haven't held it against me."

"Possibly I have, a little, Roger, but coming back to thank me . . . well, that balances everything, and adds a great deal more."

"Another of your boys *won't* be back, not right away, at least; but I know he's grateful, too. He told me so, so I'm going to talk for him until he comes back and can talk for himself. I mean Andrew."

Andrew was a colored boy who had posed special problems. His sins both of omission and commission had been many. I could understand his rebellion against virtually everything. I did know that he came from a good religious home.

"Andrew," I said to him one day, "you're young, and of course you don't expect anything to happen to you—like dying, for instance. But suppose something *did* happen— and right when it happened you were doing something wrong?"

I was not too sure that he had understood me, so I repeated the same words later on, several times, possibly. One must repeat often with the retarded. I hoped they were noted and filed away in Andrew's mind.

"You know, if you studied and learned, Andrew," I told him another time, "I believe you could become a very good preacher."

I remembered these two bits of counseling the instant Roger mentioned Andrew's name. Roger continued.

"Several times Andrew told me what you said to him," said Roger, "about how would he feel if something happened—dying, you meant—and he was doing something wrong at the time. He told me he never forgot the times you said that to him. And you know where he is now? He's away studying to be a preacher."

It was a little thing, but a big thing, that Roger came to tell me about Andrew and himself, proving to me in a simple and powerful way the value of my humble techniques.

When Roger left, I sat back and had a few golden-hour memories for those who had studied with me, and left me, to fill their simple niches, but proudly, in the world beyond school.

Jean, they said, would never even learn to read. Well, she has not graduated yet, not from school, that is, but she has left my class. She reads, and avidly, everything she can draw from the juvenile section of the department store bookshop. I have no fear for any child who can read, for reasons that I have given several times, the principal of which is: reading is the key to the world's knowledge. Abraham Lincoln read his way to the Presidency of the United States.

Charles was a strange child. He managed to get out of virtually all school work. I regarded him as one of my few failures, until he, like Roger, returned to me one day. He is married, he told me, and has a child.

"I should have listened to you," he said. *"My boy is going to knuckle down and make something of himself. When I was in your class I knew more than you did. Now, I can't pass the examination for my driver's license, because I can't read the rules. So I keep renewing my beginner's license. My son shall learn to *read*. I'm doing all right, but I'm here to apologize to you for not doing *better*, and to thank you for trying to get the truth through my thick skull."

Strange gratitude for apparent failure.

I remembered George, Melvin, and Eugene. These three have worked as bus boys, and behind the counters of industry, for years. They have always been dependable. Melvin has had the same job for fifteen years, owns an $8000 home and a car, and is seldom absent from his work.

Then, there is a magazine store and a shoeshine stand which I would visit oftener if I were not afraid its owner would think I am imposing.

Sam works at this place. I did not know that. Sam did not come to me to say thanks. Maybe it did not occur to him. Maybe I just happened to go into the place on this particular day. Possibly it was not even chance.

"You are Mrs. Smith, the teacher," said the proprietor. He did not ask me, he told me.

"Why, yes, yes I am," I said. "How did you know?"

"Sam pointed you out on the street. He often talks about you."

"Sam? Sam who?"

"This Sam was in your class. He keeps telling me you did all kinds of good for him."

"I'm afraid I still do not understand."

The smiling, happy, enthusiastic Greek owner of the store must have thought me somewhat stupid.

"Sam works for me," he explained. "He is the best I have ever had. He sells magazines, and customers like him, keep coming back. He shines shoes, and customers like his work, and come back and ask for Sam."

He was so effusive I felt myself flushing. I could not believe I had done this well by Sam, whom of course I now remembered as one of my recent graduates.

I noticed, among the other items for sale in that store, that the owner roasted and sold peanuts. I do not particularly care for peanuts, but the proprietor—Sam was not in at the time—noting the direction of my gaze, hurried and filled a big bag with them.

"No, no," he said, "you do not pay for these! I make you a present of them, because I am so thankful to you for Sam!"

I do not return to that particular store. Possibly I should, but I might embarrass Sam, if he is in, and I feel I must be careful, lest Sam's employer think he must give me peanuts regularly!

XIV

Operation Retard

RETARDATION is not the fault of the retarded, yet the so-called
"normal" of all ages seem to blame them for their condition.
As soon as the different child realizes something of his
difference, which is heartbreakingly early in life, he sets
himself apart. He does it even before other people start it—
though some doctor or other scientist may note some difference ahead even of the child.

Children, we have been told, are naturally cruel. Certainly
they are intolerant and thoughtless. But in my experience
they are not more so than adults, even the parents of the so-
called "retarded" child. I say "so-called" advisedly, since
fifteen years have shown me, during my dedication to
slow learners, that one can not be so sure a child is severely
retarded.

Look with me at my eighteen pupils again, half boys, half
girls. Look back with me in imagination if you can, to last
year's class, from which the usual percentage were promoted
and so passed out of my class, but not out of my heart and
my life. Year before last there were others, and so on back
to the first tremulous time I faced the retarded, noted the
still, or drawn, or reserved, or fearful expressions on their
faces, and knew that I had found my niche. My pupils, I

tried to make clear to them without putting the thought into words, had found a champion.

I had majored in special education. There was much interest, academically, in special education at all levels. Children who were slow learners were assigned to special classes; children not so slow, save in certain departments, were assigned to remedial classes. I rebelled at once against any semblance of segregation. "Remedial" might do, but "special," never! But in my early teaching days, theories had to be followed. Older heads knew better than I.

I had to do some talking to substitute "Mrs. Smith's Class," with my name on the door—exactly as teachers' names appeared on the doors of normal classrooms to the right and left of mine—but my reports to state educational headquarters always refer to my class as special.

But think a moment. Every remembered day of a child's life has been special. Every day of the slow one's life has been filled with:

"I don't know why you have to be told over and over how to do the simplest things!" this from the exasperated mother or father. "Your brothers and sisters are as bright as anybody."

Or:

"I don't know what I ever did to deserve such a *dull* child!"

Even if the retarded child does not understand the words, he is even more adept than the dog or cat in realizing the deprecatory undertones or overtones of daily speech. Can't he learn? He begins to believe he can not, otherwise, why would his own mother say he can't? Is he dull? Mother says so, father said so last night, and they have both taught him to honor and obey and trust his parents. Of course they become irritated and lose patience with him, but it must be his fault, since they could not possibly be wrong; parents couldn't.

Or:

"You're pretty dumb, aren't you?" This from some schoolmate or neighbor's child. "My people say you're so dumb you don't have good sense. I'd go hide my head if I were you."

This is not at all uncommon, as every one who faces facts knows. It is not uncommon for normal children to chase and jeer at the slow learner. I have seen such frightened children running from the laughing, hilarious mob, as a terror-stricken one might flee from known lynchers. And the comparison is apt, for while the lyncher slays only the body of his victim, if he can catch him, the mental lyncher leaves the body alive, and slowly, through all his lifetime, lynches the mind—and even the spirit—of the so-called retarded.

We all assume attitudes of superiority. Certain people bore us. If we feel that we are people of intelligence, we spare no time for the person who is slow of speech, whose mental pictures are too simple to interest us, whose words are difficult to understand. By our attitude toward others are we judged by God Almighty, of this I am sure. Others seldom judge us by this attitude, simply because the attitude is so widespread.

How can we assess this for ourselves? A few chapters back I suggested that the reader test himself by reading my simple words aloud. By his facility, or his stumbling, he discovers—possibly to his surprised humiliation—that he reads at a level much lower than he had ever imagined.

What, reader, is your attitude toward the retarded child, aside from the relief you have felt every time one of your own children grew into intelligence, that there was "nothing wrong with the child"? I do not ask whether you go out of your normal way to assume an attitude to a slow child. I only ask this: if an obviously slow child asks you a simple question, how do you answer that child? Do you answer him, or her, if you bother to answer at all, as you would answer one of your own children—if your children are normal—or do you mumble, talk down, or pretend you do not hear? And if the retarded child is your own son or daughter, do you spend as little time as humanly possible helping that child to find himself, herself? Do you actually abuse that child by your attitude, you who would not think of beating him or her with a cat-o'-nine-tails?

Take care, father, mother! That retarded child came to be your teacher, to show you, mutely, how to make spiritual progress. Hide behind your newspaper from questions, father, hide behind a noisy vacuum cleaner, mother, and be sure of this: the Father knows where you are hiding, and that child He sent you is His messenger! If this sounds extreme, so be it. When it comes to the rehabilitation of retarded children—and one-fifth of our yearly average in elementary schools must be called retarded—I am a zealot and I believe we need, around the nation, more and more zealots in the same educational areas.

I look at my eighteen children. One of them, Edith Z., "completely anti-social," called to me just before class and said: "On my way to school I heard one of the teachers on the bus talking. She's one of the teachers at the Plum school. She said to some lady: 'If that Rodney Gray in my room doesn't do better I'll have to try to send him over to that class of Mrs. Smith's. He's such a dumbbell.' " Then she added: "What did she mean? Did she mean us?" I told her that there were several Mrs. Smiths teaching in our schools. This seemed to satisfy her. I am shocked that this teacher, a good friend of mine, can have so forgotten herself as to make such a remark.

The probable consequences are these: others besides Edith may have heard and will instantly spread the story that pupils in "Mrs. Smith's Class" are dumbbells. Edith herself, unless I make sure she does nothing of the sort, will spread it in the class. Each class member will go home and ask his parents if his fellow pupils and himself *are* dumbbells. Nothing travels like a loathsome piece of "truth."

I recalled my first faculty meeting at this school, with a new principal, who said: "This is my first year here. I believe it is also Mrs. Smith's. Here is something for all of you to keep in mind: I do not know much about special education, but I do know human needs. As long as I am here I want Mrs. Smith's group to be included in everything and never referred to as special or in any derogatory manner." That principal's attitude, bless him, set the pattern that still exists in my school. Unfortunately, it does not exist in all schools in the district.

I knew what I was going to do, just what I have always done in like cases. I would make sure that Edith had told the truth, while praying that she had not. I did not wish her to be proved a liar, but lying on the part of one person, and destructive, wide-traveling remarks on the part of one in authority, leave a simple choice. I can deal with one person. Once contagion spreads, epidemics must be contained.

I called Edith back to me.

"You're quite sure you heard that teacher say what you just told me?"

Her eyes were red with unshed tears.

"I'm sure, Mrs. Smith. Not only that, she saw me when she said it, and knew I heard every word."

"Hush, now, you can't know that's true!"

Was I helping a child to spread gossip? Was I doing the right thing in pumping Edith? I was getting at the truth in the only way I knew. I must be sure. I knew the lady Edith had not identified, another teacher friend of mine; they rode the bus together. At the first opportunity, which was a joint meeting of the teachers of the various schools, I made it a point to see them.

"Did either of you say in the bus last week that my class consisted of dumbbells?"

At first they said they had not, but when I gave a detailed account of what Edith had told me, one of them said: "Marion, God help me, I did say that. I lost control of my temper. Rodney has been such a difficult child. I didn't say it in front of any one, but someone must have heard, or you'd not know about it now. What can I do to make it right?"

"Nothing, except never do it again and make sure you don't say it to the children in your class. You can't go around telling the school that my children *aren't* dumbbells, or the children will wonder why you protest so much. Please be careful about what you say. Years of good public relations work have made my class an accepted one. A few ill-chosen words can do irreparable damage."

We agreed to try. But weeks passed before Edith got over it. She learned as much from it, however, as did the teacher and myself. She learned what harm a small word could cause. It helped bring her out of her own anti-social tendencies. But that the word "dumbbell" did some good in this instance was purely coincidental.

I am against segregation in any manner, or any suggestion of it. Not all educators have formed their opinions, either way, on the subject of segregation. I feel that elimination of segregation and a practical approach to educating the retarded are two things that we need in order to educate these children successfully to the place where they will be capable, confident, contributing, taxpaying adults of the future.

XV

Small Slow Soldiers

PUT a naturally slouchy man into uniform and he straightens up like a soldier. Dress him in white tie and tails and he walks with pride. Shine his shoes and he is conscious of his spruceness. This is true of all men, all women. It has been established time after time in the uniformed services. Men and women in snappy uniforms are themselves snappy, and straight-marching. Men and women in fatigues or unpressed uniforms assume the slouch, the sprawl their lack of tidiness seems to indicate.

I knew this long before I began teaching the retarded. When I knew I was going to devote my teaching life to the slow learner I made up my mind to use good appearance as a key to personality. Both good appearance and bad attract the attention of others. The slow, to have the proper breaks, must always attract the best attention; the head-nodding kind, not the bemused, head-shaking kind.

Far too many of my class reach me the first time somewhat disheveled. I do not mean on the initial visit, when children's parents just naturally dress them up, so that they make a good impression, but the first time they really come to school, to spend that first all-important day.

As far as I am concerned, when a child comes to me he has come to have his clothing fitted, his hair combed, his teeth brushed, his shoes shined. He has come to make a new start.

I know from long experience that my work with that child must be gradual. If I try to make a child's appearance entirely over during his first day, or even his first week with me, I stand an excellent chance of being visited by an irate parent demanding that she be at once informed what is wrong with Johnny, or Janet. Do I imply that he is dirty, that her hair is matted, that his shoes are too big, that she never washes her teeth? I avoid all this. My daily tasks are sufficiently demanding.

I work carefully and diplomatically on individuals, spending considerable time on the class as a whole, sometimes using individuals, who need more careful instruction, as examples. Only I know that there is a method behind this use of examples.

Every classroom in my building has a clothes closet. It has several doors, all of which open at once, from a central control at one end of the closet. The closet is equipped with hooks. Children are supposed to hang up their hats, coats, mufflers, and place their galoshes directly below their own garments. I explain the use of the closet to the class. Yes, I know this is simple, and fundamental, but you would be surprised how few retarded children have ever been told.

"I'm going to assign one of you the task of supervising the clothes closet," I tell them. "The boy or girl who maintains the best appearance for a given week, supervises the door the following week. You children yourselves, after you know what I mean, may select the boy or girl who has made the best appearance. But it must be an honest choice. If I do not agree with you, I shall make the selection myself, and tell you exactly why. Now, you'll notice that in addition to the usual hooks, this closet is provided with coat hangers. That's important, for when a coat is neatly and carefully placed on a hanger, it fits that hanger just as neatly and smoothly as it is *supposed* to fit your shoulders. And your coat is supposed to ride neatly while you wear it. . . ."

It goes without saying that I am myself meticulous about every item of my own clothing. I use a minimum of lipstick and rouge. My hair is always exactly right before I leave my home. I make sure, without primping, that it remains that way all day. A quick touch of the hand is enough. And if a stray bun of hair slips from its moorings, my children are just as quick—but always respectfully—to call my attention to the slip as I am to correct them. We work together. If children notice my smartness, or temporary lack of it, they will note one another and themselves.

Few mothers know how to arrange their daughters' hair becomingly. And some mothers—too many—take the stand that it does not matter in school. Yet school is the preparation place for adulthood, and it is there that first impressions are the most important. It is the "keen" dresser who turns the heads of all others who may despair of emulation.

Not all of my children's parents can afford to dress their young expensively. In fact, few can. But all can dress them, if they can dress them at all, attractively. If a child has one to wear and one to wash, that child can dress attractively.

I do not expect parents to do more than decide hurriedly that a child is ready for school, give him, according to the old saying, "a lick and a promise." Then, the child is off the parents' hands until his afternoon return home. This is the common attitude.

It does vitally matter how a child appears at school. Everybody should know this, but so few people stop to think about it, *from the viewpoint of the child.* Let a poor boy go to school with patches on his pants and his whole future can be affected, because everybody in school except the most spiritually advanced, the truly sympathetic, will call the attention of everybody else to the patches. The patches are badges of poverty. And when a boy feels poor, in his innerself he *is* poor.

If the clothing is careless, so will the mind and spirit be.

So, one of the best beginning places with the slow child is his appearance. One morning I may talk about how boys should keep their hair combed. I may ask the girls to help me explain just what I mean. I may ask them to point out just which hair they find neatest among the boys. If the boys rebel I promise them that they will have a chance to comment on the girls' hairdos tomorrow. I emphasize one simple fact, however, that mean or hurting comments will not be permitted, that ladies and gentlemen never hurt one another's feelings.

Even though the girls are likely to make a game, with much laughter, out of this hair combing technique, they nevertheless pay attention. One does not have to pull a long face to be attentive. My intention is to cause every boy and girl to be aware of his hair. If a girl's hairdo can be improved —and most can, as any woman knows—I use that child as an example, *never a bad example,* mind, and I never comment adversely on any child's hairdo, or allow any pupil to do so. I simply show where, as I put it, "Mary's nice hair can be made to look even nicer" if combed or pinned a certain way. I do not want that child to go home and protest to her mother that I have made some sort of show of her before the class. I want her to boast that she has been used as an example, and so she has. I also wish the child to make the mother a bit thoughtful about the matter of appearance.

But I do not want ever to inspire the child to rush straight home and start sprucing up his or her parents! No. While this may well be the eventual result, it comes about slowly, and naturally. It is fatal to rush such matters, for parents of retarded children are touchy and, I think, understandably so. If I can not, spending my days with eighteen boys and girls, understand the harassment of parents who have one such child all the time I don't have him, then I have learned much less in fifteen years than I believe I have.

Day by day, during certain periods when the appearance of any of my pupils inspires such action, I go into the matter of shined shoes, sweaters that fit, brushed teeth, washed hands, erect walking, prideful bearing, shirttails in, shirt-waists unrumpled, coats hanging evenly on hangers. I do not hurry matters. I am happy if progress is gradual—and therefore lasting.

My "keeper of the door" of the closet has the task, or quickly assumes it, of checking on the clothes in the closet after children have, supposedly, secured their garments. He makes sure they hang straight, and that each is on its assigned hook or hanger. If he finds anything out of line, he has the authority—or assumes it—to whisper the facts to the owner of the garment or garments, who immediately makes due correction, and is subtly encouraged to remember.

One of the reasons, then, why most people cannot tell my retarded children from normal children, is that my retarded ones are as neat or neater in appearance. They have to be. They must have some common reason, however unimportant it may seem, to feel proud. Pride in dress is not vanity. It is not a crutch. Any man or woman who has ever sought employment knows how high a price employers place on personal appearance.

Carol is, day after day, one of the cutest children in not only my classroom but my big school.

Untidy John is untidy only in comparison with others in his own classroom. Nobody knows better than John himself that, beside some boys his own age in other classrooms, he is a small fashion-plate.

Jeans are for boys, and my boys wear them as neatly as jeans can be worn. I discourage jeans for the girls.

The general result is this: day after day, sometimes for two or three weeks in succession, I find nothing to criticize in the appearance of any of my pupils. The pupils themselves are acutely aware of this, because they themselves have brought about this happy result. They do not care who sees them as they are. In fact, they want people to see how well they look.

They have discovered that the clothes approach to pride in bearing is much more easily worn than spiritual retreat into personal darkness, where it matters not at all to the stricken how he is dressed.

XVI

Pressurized Children

EVERY human being is under pressure of some sort. Normal men and women in everyday life experience constant pressure which often invades their sleep, or prevents sleep. Normal children face pressures from all directions from their earliest memories. There is no use railing against this. We simply learn to manipulate such pressures to our own use. We learn to live with them. We learn to endure them as best we can. We "give" to them when and where we must.

The normal child, with some ability to reason, recognizes pressures. He rebels against them. He protests them. He runs away from them. He faces them. He fights them. But reason tells him that he must somehow manage to live with them, without being destroyed or even pained by them. The normal child's reason is, like the governor on an engine, that balancing mechanism which makes it possible for the child to live with pressures, almost all of which seem to be spiritual. Other pressures, such as physical ones, are relieved in sports and games. But the normal child gives with pressures, takes pressure, as he participates in a tug-o'-war that, in actual living, is lifelong.

So, discipline is exercised on the normal child. He is told that there are certain things expected of him. He is told that there are things he must do. He must control his urge to make more noise than his neighbor. He must control his urge to pull girls' hair. He must control his urge to kick or hit things. He must curb his urge to daydream when lessons must be studied and mastered. He must be in school at a certain time. He must remain for a certain length of time. He must move, in orderly fashion, from class to class. There is an established routine of school work and play to which he is expected to adhere. He learns this early, and reacts according to his capacity. He must learn his lessons, the pressure being that he will not graduate next year if he doesn't, or that some other boy or girl will out-do him, or the teacher will frown at him, or look at him thoughtfully, or fail him, or lecture him. If he does not do well in school he must justify his lack of progress to father, mother, or guardian. The pressure is everywhere, and all the time. As the boy or girl learns to manipulate this pressure, so does that boy or girl prepare for life.

The retarded child faces exactly the same pressure, with vastly slowed down equipment. The retarded child is expected to give or take to normal pressures, while the same child is told, from its earliest knowledge of its differences, that it is not up to it. The child already is aware that there is much abroad in the world that it does not comprehend, through which it does not move as easily and confidently as do other children. It is woefully aware that the other children know this, and point it out. It is the pointing that constitutes the worst pressure.

It is an odd fact that parents and teachers are more likely to explain carefully the whys and wherefores of discipline to the normal child, because that child understands, and responds. To the child who needs more, and more careful explanations, the parental and, too often, the educational attitude is: "No use telling you over and over again, you haven't sense enough to learn anyway."

No person knows really whether any other person, seemingly less endowed mentally, is able to learn.

Therefore, the retarded child, generally, lacks explanations for things, as if he were expected to have been born knowing. This is not expected of normal children. It is always easier to teach a normal child, therefore more time is devoted to the normal child; results are more noticeable, and the task of producing them clearly much less. Yes, teachers, in school and out, are human: they are prone to follow the lines of least resistance. Work with the normal is easier, the results more satisfying.

A retarded child asks his mother a question, any question. She ignores him, mumbles, tells him to run along and play, or answers irritably; possibly she tells him the question is silly; possibly she is too busy to answer. The retarded child is rebuffed.

"Why?" the child asks himself. "Why?"

The normal child asks these same questions, but from himself, or from someone else, he obtains answers of a sort. They may not satisfy him, but he can reason things out for himself.

The retarded child asks someone else, a neighbor, say:

"Run along and ask your father, or mother. I don't have time to answer foolish questions."

Foolish questions? What is meant by "foolish"?

Strangely enough anybody will explain this to the retarded child; the questions are foolish because the retarded child, not having been born knowing everything, is therefore a fool. His own fault, too, as he should be able to see. If he had any sense he would know better than to annoy normal, superior people with foolish questions!

"Why?" asks the retarded child. "Why?"

Maybe he tries to get answers—one time, possibly, twice improbably—from children his own age.

"Yeh, yeh, dumbbell! You don't know anything, do you? Go hide your thick head in the sand, like an ostrich!"

The parents of a child so hideously rebuffed may take such talk up with the parents of the offending children, though it is not likely. If they do this sort of response may eventuate:

"You can't blame my children for putting your child in his place. Maybe he isn't silly enough to be in an institution, but he shouldn't be allowed to mingle with brighter children."

If there are people of any sort who know, instantly, more about the mental capacity of children than doctors, surgeons, psychiatrists, and psychologists, it is parents of reputedly normal children—unless it is people who have no children at all.

So, parents put off the retarded child.

Neighbors frown at the retarded child.

Schoolmates jeer at the retarded child.

The retarded child enters a class. He must arrive on time. Why? He must sit in a certain seat. Why? He must learn to read. Why? He must get along with other people. Why? He must not take things belonging to others. Why not? He must learn good manners. Why? He must appear well. Why? He must be quiet. Why? He must be polite. Why? He must ask teacher if he may leave the room. Why? He must raise his hand if he wishes to talk to the little girl across the aisle. Why? He must not snap his fingers or yell the teacher's name to attract her attention. Why not? He must draw figures in which he has no interest. Why? He must tell the teacher what pictures mean. Why? He must hang up his coat. Why? He must pay attention. Why? He must not spend his time looking out the window, daydreaming. Why not?

From every direction there is pressure on the retarded child. If given time, he may himself grasp why this is so and that is not, but in a world manipulated by normal people faster of thought than himself, he is never given time to react. Yet somehow he must react. How? He does not know. The harder he tries to know the less he seems to know. The harder he strives to emerge from confusion, the more confused he becomes. He cannot even find words to express his reaction, because even if he had the words, he could not analyze his reactions. He wants, or he does not want, and what he wants he cannot have. What he does not want he must take.

Confusion breeds confusion, and Ted throws a tantrum which expresses nothing at all except that the pressure has been too great.

Striving to react like a normal person, George raises his hand, snaps his fingers, even screams the teacher's name.

Robert, who has tried to react "like a human being" since he discovered he was not like other human beings—not exactly like, that is—keeps his desk drawer full of candy, fruit, cakes, cookies, and eats every time the teacher turns her back. He slouches. He does not care. He is learning that if he is a hulk, and tries to be only a hulk, the waves of pressure will simply beat upon and over him. If he can lose himself in not caring, the waves will wash over him and disappear. If they do not, he can pretend they do, which is almost as good. He has found that a vacuous expression causes most people to veer off. He maintains that vacuous expression, even when he hears people say he is "dull of face and behavior." He does not give to pressure, he just ignores it. With an I.Q. of 63 he should be able to manipulate his personal pressures with comparative ease. But he needs to have them explained to him, and he needs to be encouraged to want to manipulate them to his own ends.

John, my one untidy one, has been nagged at because of his appearance. He has been nagged so much, since he could remember, that he has arrived at one inescapable conclusion: he will be nagged at no matter what he does, says, or does not do or say; so what does it matter whether he does anything? He becomes untidy. He is sullen in the face of pressure. He is rebellious in the face of pressure if it continues. He is cruel by turns, noisy, dull, by turns. Eventually, if he never understands the pressures, if they are never reasonably made clear to him, he will become incorrigible. I make up my mind at once that while I cannot relieve John of life's pressures, he will be informed of their meaning and the reason for them. No child of mine, tidy or untidy, shall have any excuse for incorrigibility.

Peter must react somehow. He is bigger than most boys of his age. Accidentally or otherwise he learns that he is much stronger, that other boys avoid him through fear, that girls exclaim over his size and strength, or run from him, screaming. He reacts to pressure by twisting the arms of the nearest smaller boys, by pulling the hair of the girls. They react in a way that Peter, at this stage of his growth—which can be most unpromising if he is not taken in hand by the understanding—finds gratifying. Peter responds sadistically to pressure. I make it clear to Peter that his strength and size were not given him as instruments to cause pain or destruction. I find a use for his size and strength, and hunt the reasons for his reaction to pressure. Peter, with an I.Q. of 67, can reason, so I reason with him.

"If someone larger than you are twisted your arms behind your back, would you like it?"

That is a simple abstraction, and Peter grasps it.

Possibly I assign Peter "administrative" tasks, explaining their importance carefully, and hold Peter responsible for results. Possibly I make him a sort of helper. It is certain that I will remove the pressure from those unpromising sadistic tendencies. Peter, without explanation from someone he senses he can trust, does not entirely control his urge to sadism; he does not try very hard. As he grows older, and pressures increase, he will try less and less. Eventually, he will seriously maim someone, perhaps even kill. This often happens in the world outside school; because someone has grown to manhood or womanhood without even understanding the normal pressures which the retarded must also face. Every human being who reaches manhood or womanhood with abnormal reactions to pressure undetected is the responsibility of the so-called "normal" public, and this responsibility is compounded, rather than fulfilled, when the undetected one goes to prison for life, is hanged, electrocuted, or killed in the gas chamber.

In the language of the boxing ring, which most men and women in this television age understand, normal children are equipped to learn for themselves how to "roll with the punches." Retarded children must be helped to learn, to a much greater extent than normal children.

It is simple, really. The teacher—parent, neighbor, schoolmate, instructor, school official—simply recognizes the slowness of the equipment of the retarded child, and slows down to match it; having slowed down, he speeds up slowly, *bringing the retarded child up to normal speed with him.*

Of course, it takes time; patience is required; and the general reaction of the normal person to this requirement, is this:

"Why should *I* waste my time? It isn't *my* child!"

Or, possibly it is the speaker's child, whereupon the answer may be:

"Stop asking silly questions!" or, "Ask your father when he comes home."

The father's response, when he comes home, is likely to be:

"Ask your mother, child! I didn't come home from a hard day at the office to face a barrage of silly questions!"

The natural reaction of the retarded child is to seek relief from normal pressures in a normal way—by asking questions. Too many adults sit stolidly, rebelliously, resentfully on the blow-off cocks, their attitudes smug as they say, or think:

"What has it to do with me? *My* kids are bright enough. And I pay my taxes, don't I?"

XVII

Leashes

TAKE a normal class, any normal class. The teacher has her head bowed at her desk, reading something, correcting examination papers. Every boy in this class, and every girl, has an I.Q. of 90 or above. Most are average normal, many are superior. One of the superior boys, sure that the teacher will not see, raises his hand to his mouth, cups it in a way boys know, and whispers to the superior girl who sits behind him.

"Mina! Did you get the answer to that last problem?"

Mina, who knows she is not supposed to answer, or hear, says:

"I've got it, yes."

"Let me see."

It happens all the time, every time the teacher's head is bowed, or her back is turned at the blackboard, or she is out of the room. It is a stark violation of discipline. Enlarge it a little in the world of adults, and it breaks the law. It calls for punishment. It calls for punishment in the world of childhood, too, so that children will know. But it passes unnoticed, often because the teacher saves herself trouble by not noticing. It is illegal. It is "school-criminal."

Bobby, average normal, digs his elbow into the ribs of

Joseph, superior. Joseph kicks back. There is a crash as his foot hits something giving off noise.

"Who did that?" says the teacher, lifting her head, her eyes accusing.

Nobody answers. Half the others know. They all connive. It is a conspiracy against authority.

"Elizabeth, who made that noise?"

There it is, the challenge direct. Elizabeth says she does not know. She knows. She lies, frankly, freely. There is a code. Elizabeth lives up to it. She does not "squeal" or "rat" or "tattle."

Bob tosses a note to Harriet. Harriet swallows it when she has finished reading it. It does not amount to anything. But it violates authority.

Somebody makes a whistle. He whistles on it, piercingly, but is apparently deeply immersed in a book when the teacher looks up.

"Jason, did you make that noise?"

"Noise, ma'am, what noise! I was so wrapped up in my studies. . . ."

More lies. Everybody knows they are lies. But Jason "gets away with it."

Somebody throws spitballs. Somebody ducks head to eat apples or oranges under the desk.

It happens all the time. Somebody makes noise. If nobody says anything, the noise increases. Give a normal child a mile, he takes ten miles. Teacher leaves room. Chalk or marbles pelt the blackboard. In seconds the place is in an uproar. Teacher returns. No use trying to find out who started it. Code, the code of childhood, immutable, like the laws of the Medes and Persians. One noise calls for more noise, more noise calls for bedlam, until sudden silence is brought by the teacher, or the principal, or someone else in authority.

Only, it is difficult to allay bedlam with the slow learner. He is as slow to stop as to get started, unless . . .

Unless there are leashes, held in accustomed, efficient hands. I have eighteen pupils, most of the school year, in my class. Each one must be reached before he can leave my class.

Jane calls out something. It does not much matter what. It gives Mary a stronger idea and she calls out, too. That makes others call out. Bedlam ensues unless . . .

Unless the leash I hold on Mary is quickly pulled. It is not a real leash. It never could be. And nobody would want it, least of all Mary, or myself.

But the leash is there. It cannot be detached from Mary. "Mary! You're first. What do you want?"

I am not accusing her, not exercising authority. I am answering her outcry, as if she had held up her hand to ask something. She is asking something, but she is detouring authority; she is asking without realizing that she asks.

"Children! Quiet! Mary has a question!"

It works. Spur of the moment things have to work. They cannot become routine, stereotyped, not with the slow learner. He often has to be surprised.

Often my class seems like a slice of bedlam to a visitor, someone in the outside hall, when the door is open. But I have ways. An arched eyebrow. A stern face. Insistence on being heard. Clapped hands. There is something about clapping the hands, teacher's hands, that works if not done too frequently. One must never cry wolf. The retarded knows the cry-wolf idea, though he may never have heard the story, or understood it if he heard. Too much of an abstraction. But he learns quickly enough that the clapping hands, which sound so much like spanking hands, do not actually spank. Between clappings he must be allowed to forget, so that each clapping will be a surprise.

It could seem that all my eighteen are puppets on strings. I allow them movement, and sound, within range of their leashes. The leashes are invisible. They are not unusual. There are leashes on all of us in the world of the adult, so children should become accustomed to them.

Speed limits are leashes. Laws are leashes. Honor is a leash. Truth is a leash. Time is a leash. Everybody lives by leashes, so do not get the idea that my students are trained to be animals. They are trained to be human beings on the stage of life.

Paul cannot sit still. He gets up without permission, strides and sits at the desk with someone else, rises, goes to someone else. He has the room in turmoil, all too quickly.

When Paul rises, without permission, I say:

"Go right on out the door and stand in the hall until I call you. Be there when I call. You'll return only when you can stay in your seat, or ask permission."

Paul responds to his leash. He knows the leash is there. He likes and trusts me because I tighten it. He knows I will not forget him in the hall. He will play square and wait out there until I call him. He will not intrude at the doors of other classrooms. They have already been forever closed against him, or he would not be in my class. Forever? No, not if I can rehabilitate him, when I can rehabilitate him. I am his hope. He does not word it like that, think it like that, but he knows it. He does not wish to escape my leash.

The leash on Carol is kind, but firm. She becomes rattled, and reverts to her first speech, which only Carol and Ned understood—and possibly their two mothers. When Carol becomes excited—she always has a small frown on her face —I call her to me.

Enroute to the desk she stops talking, keeps on frowning, but is herself when I say to her:

"What were you saying?"

Whatever it was, and it does not have to be the same thing at all, she says it clearly now. I have pulled her to me with the leash of our mutual understanding. I have, in a fashion, choked off her incoherent speech, opened the channels of her understandable speech. Leash for Carol.

My leash on Edith is hooked up to her principal attribute, her anti-sociability. She does not like anyone, but she feels it terribly if anyone fails to like her, or at least tolerate her. When Edith begins frowning at people, and I know she is about to express herself in a way that will start bedlam again, and cause her loss of class liking, I tweak the leash.

"Edith, will you come here a moment?"

My voice tells her I have something important for her to do. She comes forward. I assign her a task. She forgets whatever it was that disturbed her. She holds it in abeyance, which is the best most of us do with our pressures.

Three or four boys like to sit together. They like to have fun together during class. Studies are not important to them. I let them sit together, but they must be able to show results from cooperation or I separate them. They must earn the right to sit together. They try, they try hard.

My strongest leash is the project.

Projects are class or group efforts. They involve cooperation, and more time than class operations. They are self-operating leashes, fastened to individuals and groups by time—the time required to make a project something visible, tangible, and according to the original plan everybody in the class knows.

I leash my groups together for an hour at a time, intent on doing their share of a given project.

That gives me time for work with individuals who have not yet fitted into any group. This is more of an individual leash. It is tied to the chair beside my desk. A boy or girl sits in it, close to me, "tied" to me. I ask that child questions, or he asks me questions. We work together. The leash is not visible, but it is there. My leashes connect with every child.

I must always know the exact point at which to tweak a leash. My class must never be allowed to get out of hand.

It is a tiring business, clinging all through a school day to eighteen leashes attached to boys and girls, all pulling in different directions. But no man or woman incapable of enduring fatigue of this kind, *understanding and patient fatigue,* has any business teaching the retarded—though incapable ones may learn from the retarded.

How does one regain energy, when it is being drained out out all the day long?

I regain so much of mine, almost all of it, during my blue hour, when I tot up the day's score and realize that I have accomplished something. I have made progress. Maybe it was just a little, with just one child, possibly Edith, or Mary, or Robert. But progress with even one is personal progress.

My class is noisy, to just the limit of noisiness I permit. There I tweak this leash or that one, silencing, gradually, the noisiest. Or maybe I have to tweak all leashes to restore complete order—for the few minutes true order, among the retarded, is possible.

Does it sound like a madhouse?

Not if you did not know I speak of the slow, the retarded.

Every normal class goes berserk when the teacher's back is turned, or she, or he, is out of the room. One does not regard even the noisiest as not quite balanced mentally. No, one knows by the I.Q.'s that one need not worry about mental imbalance, even if, momentarily, the classroom is a bedlam.

But the same thing in "Mrs. Smith's Class"? That is different. Those children are different. Whatever they do must be regarded with suspicion. They are not normal children. They are not even average children. That means that they must walk the chalkline more sedately, or the noisiest of normal children will regard them as "not quite all there."

So, I keep my leashes handy, always within reach, lest one child get out of line and create a wrong impression of everybody in the class, including me, since the teacher must of necessity take on some of the coloring of her work—if she is dedicated to it. If she is not, it is not her work, however hard she tries, however tired she makes herself.

My leashes are longer when I take my children out of the schoolroom on some project; to the movies, to the circus, to a dairy farm, to a greenhouse. I hold the leashes more loosely, and I call on the more responsible to help me. It works nicely. They are all little ladies and gentlemen.

Then, there are times when we go abroad in the fields, where none but ourselves can see us, when I roll up my invisible leashes, tuck them away in my heart, and free the children of all restraint.

It is touchingly remarkable how well-behaved they are.

XVIII

News of the Day

No ONE likes to be left out of things. Many normal persons feel themselves left out, as a result of which the offices of psychiatrists are filled with the frustrated. By the very nature of the individual, the retarded child is left out. He begins by leaving himself out. Let one adult refuse to answer his questions, or evade answering, or rebuff him, and he withdraws. It is this withdrawal which starts him on the road not only to uselessness but to indigence.

The retarded child must feel himself a part of his family, his school, his community. He becomes, otherwise, the lost lamb for whom the Good Shepherd seeks the most carefully.

There are many ways to make the child one with the community, the nation. He is one with the school when he is not a pupil in a segregated class. We may say that all classes are segregated by the mere fact of being classes. Certainly the first grade is segregated from the second and the third, elementary school from junior high, high school from college. But every child knows that, by exerting enough personal pressure, or riding the wave of pressure exerted by friends and relatives, he may attain to classes presumably higher than his own. From all of this the retarded is likely to feel himself shut out.

I open the doors to him in every way that comes to hand. It is a constant grasping at improvisations—as it is in day-by-day living. It is no more hit or miss than life.

I write something on the blackboard. It can be something out of a book all the class is reading. But it need not be, so long as it uses words with which all are familiar or with which they must become familiar to read at their several levels.

One of my standbys is the daily news. My children may talk little with their parents, their schoolmates, their neighbors, other children on their blocks. But they hear the speech of their elders, they listen to the radio and view television. The latter two especially are excellent avenues of escape from self; listening, and viewing. They can forget the world and its incomprehensible pressures. But while listening and viewing they hear many things they cannot possibly understand.

I try to tell them. I find what I wish to tell them in the headline news of the day. I find material in the stories of sacrifice, heroism, greed, brutality, of the day. They do ask questions about matters they hear, which become matters of much greater moment, to them, if they are shut off from answers, but I do not emphasize the evil which the land always seems to produce.

Some of this evil, which causes the endless death toll on our highways, is grist for my mill. One day most of my slow ones are going to drive. Some of them already do, secretly or openly. They need to know about safe driving.

Carefully I print certain facts on the blackboard, relative to safe driving. This is a community matter, a national matter, and thus I explain it. I ask my class if they can read what I have written. Most hands go up, and I pick one or two to read. Then I ask individuals to explain the meaning of what I have written. This they always enjoy, even the give and take of criticism from their fellows—on all of which I must maintain that leash I have already mentioned. I then have all of them print, or write—depending on their progress—what I have written on the board. I have them do it again with word builders. I ask them, repeatedly, what it means to them. I ask them if they notice how people drive. I ask them if people with whom they ride drive carefully. Thus, and simply, they become aware of many community things.

They become aware that corners are dangerous, even when there are stop signs—if people in cars, or walking, disregard them. They should always take care when they walk, be courteous and considerate when they drive. They note cars, and drivers.

But I have not finished. I have scarcely begun. Having made sure that all I have written is recorded in several ways on their papers and in their heads and hearts, I now record it semi-permanently on brown-paper scrolls affixed to easel-type bulletin boards. I print the same words, while the class calls out the words as I print, on the first big page of paper, in big letters, so that none need miss. I then leave this for all to see, and erase from the blackboard, which then becomes available for whatever I do next.

The record, however, remains on the bulletin board until the next day. There may be other items. A national election is perfect, for its details tell a story, and the young are always avid for stories. They follow an adult story as eagerly as they do the juvenile ones.

Each day's news, condensed to the comprehension of my class, fills as many pages of the bulletin board as may be necessary. When my pupils have learned, they can discuss the news with anybody, certainly as intelligently as can the average headline reader! And the knowledge that they can do this stiffens their small backs with confidence.

The next day, there is more news. I do not review yesterday's news just now. I thrust today's news in ahead of the review, to make sure that it can be remembered—again as well as or better than the headline reader remembers.

Whatever the principal items are, I reduce them to their bare bones, their simplest words, and make sure that my children know them, can read them on the blackboard. They put the story together with paper and pencil, written or printed, at their desks. They build the words with their word builders.

I then take them to the bulletin board, and ask: "Who remembers yesterday's news?" They are all always eager to show me what they remember; more eager still to prove it to one another. They read off yesterday's news, all the more eager because they do not, this time, have to write or print it, or build it.

I then turn yesterday's pages. To all intents and purposes *my* yesterday's newspaper is as dead as newsmen say yesterday's newspaper always is. But I keep mine. I do not leave it on a bus seat, a train seat, or in the car; throw it out the window, burn it, or sell it for cash. I keep it.

On a fresh sheet I set down today's news. Tomorrow it also is turned over, but kept.

At the end of the week I ask the class this:

"Which one of you believes he, or she, can start with Monday's news and repeat it to me, all through the week?"

Few can. All think they can, which is important. I ask them to tell me. I then turn back to Monday's news. There they see their mistakes of memory. There they read again news that the world, most likely, has forgotten. They begin to master the mosaic, the pattern, of community and world events. They may find history dull, dry; history they themselves live is never dry.

"All history happened exactly as these daily things happen," I explain to them. "And every last one of us has a hand in making news, and history."

"How do we know these things?" a girl asks.

"From the newspapers," I tell them. "From the radio. From television."

"How do those newspapers, radio, and television get the news?" I am then asked.

"By telegraph from all over the world. By teletypewriter from places where news is gathered by newsmen of newspapers, radio, and television."

"Is it possible for us ever to see how news comes in?"

If I lead my small ones carefully, sooner or later one of them will ask just such all-important questions. I can, of course, say this:

"Some day, when you're older, maybe you'll be able to visit a newspaper office, or a radio station, or a television station, and see for yourselves just how it is done."

Yes, I can do it this way, for it is the easy way. It is the way parents and far too many teachers may do it. It is not enough for my class.

"I'll see if I can't arrange for us all to visit a newspaper office, then a radio station, then a television station."

I do some telephoning. I do some visiting, explaining to busy officials. Wherever and however I can, I arrange for my class to see and hear. If possible, and if it is possible I make persistently sure of it, my students participate in what they see. They watch a newspaper being made. They see broadcasts being aired, watch the actors, commentators, see how disks are used. They see the busy, noisy teletypewriters in action. They have something to discuss at home—with enthusiasm that only the thoughtless will dampen with reproof.

I seldom tell people where I visit with my children that they are retarded. If the children behave well, and they cannot tell, it is a small triumph. If the children get out of hand they will simply shrug and remember their own days of getting out of hand—with nostalgia, perhaps.

It is not always possible for visitors to participate wholly in newspapers, radio, television, but my pupils, *because they can see, hear, feel, touch, smell,* learn more about matters I show them, and have officials of the activities show them, than they could ever get from spoken explanations not illustrated by sight. And then, when I write on the board, transfer to the bulletin board, have them print, write, or build, every bit of it has meaning. Mary has decided she wants to work on a newspaper, doing anything. I explain to her, and so to all of them, that reading, writing, arithmetic, geography, history, spelling, must all come first. Without knowing these they cannot work for newspapers, radio, television.

Paul explains, eagerly, that he already works on a newspaper. Outside of school hours he is a newsboy. Only, when he came to the class he could not read his own newspapers. Now he can, and he is flushed with pride that he can.

Sooner or later I make it possible for my class to participate in every community activity open to them, or that I can open to them: YWCA, YMCA, Red Cross, Community Chest, Boy Scouts, Girl Scouts.

The principal lack of the slow child is the feeling of belonging. I make sure that every one of mine belongs, and knows beyond the shadow of doubt that he belongs.

By radio, television, the newspaper, hearsay, and my bulletin board, he absorbs the news, and is curious enough about at least some of it to retain it—which is all that the average reader does.

I retain used bulletins until my class has outgrown them, before I discard them. By that time all that was important in them has been printed on the remembrance of my pupils, *all* of my pupils—at least the words of the bulletins. They are thus led subtly to realize that they live life right along with the normal. And some of them can comprehend that they live it more in detail, and thus more vitally.

XIX

Confident Paul

"I can write my name," said Paul. "That's enough."

"You're sure it's enough?" I pressed him.

"It's all my father can do, and he doesn't worry about anything, not even taxes."

"How does that happen?"

"He's on relief. I'll be on relief as soon as I can be. Never have to work."

"But you're a newsboy now, working like everybody else should work, to amount to something in the world. You can't read your own newspapers. And how do you make change?"

"Making change is easy. I can make change for a nickel or a dime. Most people have the pennies. Almost nobody ever asks for more change than for a dime. If anybody has more it's too much trouble anyway. I send him to another newsboy."

"Suppose there isn't any other newsboy?"

"I hold out a handful of money, let the buyer make his own change. Blind dealers do it all the time, and some stands only leave cigar boxes, so people will make their own change."

"And you trust everybody to do that?"

"I know who to trust. I know inside me who to trust."

"And does nobody ever take advantage of you?"

"I'm too smart!"

"Paul," I insisted, groping for some way past his strange self-assurance, "you can't be sure who will and who won't cheat you. Why even *I* might. . . ."

"No, not you. Not ever."

"But I'm practically a stranger to you."

"Yes, but I *know*."

Then and there I embarked on an unusual and possibly dubious route to the rehabilitation of Paul. I wrote this on a piece of paper:

"Please spank me, *hard*."

I tendered it to Paul. "Here," I said, "sign this, if you trust me."

Paul signed, with a flourish. He was proud of his ability to write his name, and to recognize it in whatever form he saw it. He needed no more. The road to more learning, according to Paul, was cluttered with "baby stuff." Who cared to know that "the bird is in the tree. The bird is blue. The tree is green"? Not Paul. If he could not start at the top he would simply mark time until he was old enough to leave school. Then he would continue to be a newsboy. Failing that he would go on relief and stay there. He would not even have to think. Thinking did not make his head ache, so long as he did not have to think about things like reading, spelling, arithmetic, geography. Paul behaved himself in class. He listened attentively. But he did not offer to do anything. No matter how I talked with him, he was adamant. His name, change for a dime, relief; it was a kind of litany.

I put the signed paper aside for later use, and meanwhile worked on another idea. Not a dime idea, but a quarter. It required the help of a friend at the nearest drugstore soda fountain. I saw her first, told her a little about Paul. Paul, meanwhile, had shown considerable generosity. He liked his schoolmates—whom he largely regarded as "babies," and they liked him—and they liked him all the better because he bought them candy, cakes, ice cream.

After I had prepared the woman at the soda fountain I called Paul forward.

"Do you have a quarter?" I asked him.

"Yes," he said, handing me one.

"But you don't know how to make change for a quarter, which is twenty-five cents," I pointed out to Paul. "So I'll make change."

I put aside seventeen cents, while Paul watched with interest. I rolled up eight cents in a piece of paper bearing Paul's name.

"I want you to get twenty-five cents' worth of ice cream for me, Paul," I said. "Do you mind using your own quarter?"

"I'd like to get you a quarter's worth of ice cream," said Paul.

I tendered him the seventeen cents. He appeared to have forgotten the other eight cents. I had talked about twenty-five cents, and so far as he was concerned, the seventeen cents added up to a quarter.

He went to the soda fountain to which I carefully directed him. My friend there was waiting.

"I want a quarter's worth of ice cream," said Paul, importantly.

"Yes, sir," said my woman friend.

She prepared the ice cream in a carton.

Paul gave her the seventeen cents. He picked up the carton.

"Just a moment, young man," said the woman. "You wanted twenty-five cents' worth of ice cream, didn't you say?"

"Yes," he would have hurried out.

"But this isn't twenty-five cents," objected my accomplice. "This is only seventeen cents. I must have eight cents more, or you'll have to leave the ice cream here."

"But my teacher said it was twenty-five cents," said Paul.

"Then she can't count," said the woman. "Somebody must have cheated her."

"Nobody could possibly have cheated her," said Paul. "She knows everything. . . ."

Then he must have remembered the nickel and three pennies I had rolled up in a paper. He could make any change for a dime. He knew eight cents when he saw it.

"How many cents do I need?" Paul asked the ice cream vendor.

She looked again at the seventeen cents. She counted it over quickly. Paul may or may not have been aware that *he* couldn't count seventeen cents.

"Eight cents missing."

Now Paul knew where the difficulty lay. By the time he returned to me he had worked himself up into a tantrum, almost. Paul considered himself too big for tantrums.

He came bursting through the door. My class lifted heads.

"You cheated me!" Paul shouted.

"How could I?" I asked. "Nobody could cheat you. Everybody in the class knows that. Come here and sit down."

Some minutes were required to get the rest of the class

back "on leash." But I had been expecting this hurricane and was prepared for it.

With difficulty I induced Paul to sit beside me. The ice cream seller had returned his seventeen cents. He pushed the money at me.

"It's only seventeen cents," he fumed. "You told me it was a quarter."

"No," I said, "but I did let you think it was a quarter. Since you didn't really know, you could think it anything you liked."

I took out the eight cents, showed him his name, told him to count it.

"I didn't steal it," I said. "See, it still has your name on it."

He counted it.

"Eight cents," he said. "Just what the woman said was missing from the twenty-five cents I *thought* I had."

I let him think it over a bit.

"Paul," I said finally, "I didn't cheat you, *but you can see that I could have.*"

"I couldn't believe that *you* would cheat me," said Paul.

"How can you possibly know who'll not *try* to cheat you? I look honest. I'm supposed to *be* honest, but if I am sure I can cheat you, and nobody will ever find it out, I may try. You can't be sure, can you, that I won't try?"

"I guess this is a kind of lesson," said Paul.

"What has happened to you here and now, where everybody knows and likes you, where you trust everybody, can happen to you pretty often when you're grown, and out of school. Just think about it a little."

He sat for a long time with the twenty-five cents on the desk before him, pushing the nickels and pennies around with his forefinger. His brow was furrowed. He might have been working something in calculus.

Finally he arrived at a decision.

"It wasn't for real," he said. "You were just trying to make me start learning. People aren't teachers. I'll live with people after I'm grown."

But he kept poking the change around.

I had accomplished a little.

I now arranged for another "accomplice," the custodian, until recent years called the janitor.

That afternoon I kept Paul after school. The custodian entered the classroom after all the pupils but Paul had left. He was carrying a paddle especially shaped for my use. Parenthetically, I have written permission from the parents to punish, by spanking, any child in my class. I almost never do it, even as a last resort. There are wiser, more efficient ways. But I had a plan here, for Paul alone, who was so confident of his stand on life, his "rolling with the punches" of life's pressures.

I called Paul from his desk. I pointed to his signature on the piece of paper.

"Whose name is this?" I asked him.

"Mine," he said proudly.

"You signed it?"

"Of course I did. You asked me to. You saw me do it."

"And what does the rest of this say? The things I wrote, what are they?"

Few people who cannot read care to give away the fact. Paul was no exception. He would not tell somebody he could not make change. He would get around it some way. Usually he sent the customer to another newsman.

"Aw," said Paul, "let *him* read it."

My little scheme was working. I had, so far, read Paul efficiently.

The custodian took the piece of paper. Slowly and carefully he read:

"Please spank me, *hard*. (Signed) Paul."

Paul looked outraged. The custodian stared at Paul. Then the custodian walked to the outer door. At the door he looked back at Paul, deadpan.

"Sucker!" said the custodian.

"It *doesn't* say that!" said Paul.

"Shall I call back the custodian?" I asked. "Or do you still trust me?"

"I trust you, outside of lessons," said Paul. Then he began to grasp the general idea, especially as I now hefted the paddle the custodian had brought me, and moved to a nearby table.

"All right, Paul," I said. "Come here to the table and bend over."

"You're not going to hold me to that . . . that . . ."

"In the world after school," I pointed out, "men hold you to whatever you have signed. Did you or didn't you sign that piece of paper?"

"I signed it," agreed Paul.

"You believe it says what the custodian said it did?"

"If you say so, yes. But for me to take a licking . . ."

"A *hard* one, it says here," I pointed out.

Paul hesitated. He was half again my size and weight. He could have taken the paddle and used it on me. His face was red with anger and something else, embarrassment, possibly, maybe humiliation. He hesitated at the table, before bending over.

"That piece of paper says 'hard'?" he asked.

"Hard!" I replied.

"Then, do it hard, as hard as you can lay it on, so I'll never forget," said Paul.

I had intended all along to go through with it, but not hard as Paul kept insisting while I laid on the paddle, confining myself to the area where it would sting plenty without causing real damage.

When I desisted—I slowed down a time or two and Paul yelled for me to paddle harder—Paul was not crying, but his face was red, and though he did not put his palms on the place where I had paddled him, I could see that he would have if I had not been watching him.

"Would you have paddled me if I hadn't agreed?" he asked.

"An agreement is an agreement, an order an order," I said.

"And outside I'd be held to anything I signed, whether or not I could read it?"

"Yes."

He managed a rueful grin.

"Let's learn to read and write and count," he said. "Especially let's learn to read and count, shall we?"

"You know where you have to start, don't you?"

"Yes," he retorted, now putting one hand back to rub himself, "I know, with that baby stuff. But let's see how fast we can get it over with!"

I was a young eager teacher when I spanked Paul. I've never spanked another child. I disapprove of corporal punishment.

I've never induced another child to sign something he did not read or understand. This story of Paul, therefore, indicates two improper actions on my part. Though they worked with Paul, I should have planned more honestly.

XX

My Last Excuse

THIS is a good place to mention my first Paul. He had long since become sixteen and gone out into the world. I had known he would never set the world on fire. But I had confidence in him. I had confidence in all of my children, and did all I could to keep track of them after they left me, either to go to work or return to graded classes and go on as far as they were capable. My children, grown to men and women, were pretty much scattered. But as far as I could learn none was indigent. If they did not pay taxes, at least they required none of my taxes, or yours, to keep them vegetatively alive.

For easily understandable reasons, my graduates did not all keep track of me. Some returned to me occasionally to report their progress, but many, mistakenly I think, preferred to forget they had found it necessary to go through a special class.

I could scarcely blame them, but I am human. I wanted to know that my results were good, enduring. If my life were being lived in vain I wanted to know before I had frittered too much of it away.

The special class, before it was known as "Mrs. Smith's Class," was always, in some fashion or other, under attack. Under attack in small ways, but under attack. For example,

I would have visitors who assumed superior attitudes simply because they knew in advance that my children were slow. I never permitted this if I could catch them before they appeared. But it was not always possible. Instantly my children knew, and were reminded of how they had been, they sensed how thin the wall might be between what they were before they came to me and after what I had done for them, and they for one another. One visitor with a superior attitude could, especially in my newest pupils, cause a fearful setback. Their lack of realization was more ignorant than the general ignorance of my slowest, but since they mirrored only the attitude of the general public, I could not blame them. I blamed myself for not catching them in time.

In one school where I taught, social segregation was evident. Normal children came and went in my classroom, bearing reports for me to initial, messages, and so forth. That they knew the nature of the special class was always apparent. Possibly my sensibilities stick out too far, but I do not think so. When a child younger than my oldest, but three or four grades advanced in school, came strutting into the classroom, and gazed at my children with disdain, then at me as if to say, "You must be a lot like 'em or you wouldn't be their teacher," I became aware of the small attacks all over again.

"Mrs. Smith, who was that girl who just came in? Is she in a higher class than this one?"

I could not lie, could not evade.

I would nod, and wait. Usually little more was said at the time, but as the hurt child turned away, a lot was thought, and a great deal more was said later on.

So, during World War II, which gave me an excellent excuse so that I did not feel guilty, I gave myself a vacation from the retarded. Women were needed in plants which produced war materials. The pay was better than I had ever received as a teacher. I turned my back on my class and went into war work.

My work was interesting but, of course, routine after I mastered it. There were several foremen in my department, men who had charge of other men whose tasks were the making of precision tools, odd items of armament, and various things in secret categories. I knew none of those things as such, but the foremen had to know them. There were six foremen. Each, according to the rules, required at least a high school education.

My job was to check work sheets, progress reports, materials allocations and prices, hours of work per man, or man-hours of work. These work sheets were prepared each day by the foremen.

Five of the foremen presented their reports in person, and sometimes chatted with me until I checked their work. They made mistakes occasionally, as their superiors had known, and expected, else there would have been no job for me.

But the sixth foreman *sent* his reports. I did not especially mind. None was required to bring them, though if I found errors it saved sending for the foreman who had made it. The sixth foreman made no mistakes, and his work was neatest of all. I was intrigued by the mystery he built up about himself.

And I had a feeling of familiarity when I noted his handwriting. When I noticed that his name was Paul I began to fumble back in memory to the various Pauls I had known. There had been several Pauls in my classes, but this job required a high school education, and none of my Pauls, as far as I knew, had ever graduated from high school.

I sent word to this Paul that I would like to see him in the office after his shift went off work. I did not wish to pull him away from his work. I also did not wish to see him in the presence of his superiors or mine. I thought I had guessed—impossible as it seemed—why he never brought his reports.

He entered the door, closed it behind him, looked at me. He did not say anything. He was my first Paul. There was no mistake. I had felt sure after checking his name and handwriting against my memories. And now he just stood, looking at me. I thought he was a little afraid.

"Hello, Paul," I said, finally.

"Mrs. Smith," he burst out, "they don't know about me here. I never want them to know."

"To know *what?*" I asked him, though of course I already knew.

"That I was ever in a special class. They'd let me go."

"You're afraid I'll tell?"

"Well, not exactly. Maybe I was, too. But now I'm not."

"Paul," I said, speaking from a suddenly full heart, "I'm so very proud of you."

He did not answer that for a few minutes. He was proud of himself, so he understood me perfectly.

"I'm glad," he said.

"Maybe I shouldn't tell you," I went on, "but your work is the neatest of all the foremen, and the most accurate."

His face brightened.

"The boss knows this?"

"Of course. It's so clear it can't be missed."

"And you didn't tell him? You didn't point it out because I was one of your pupils?"

"I pointed it out, yes," I told him.

His face fell, or started to skid.

"But I told him before I knew you were *my* Paul," I said hastily.

"*My* Paul," he repeated slowly. "Yes, you can say that. I'm something you did. If I hadn't come to you, if my people hadn't taken me to you, I'd never have this job. It's such a good one. It pays well, too."

I grinned at him. "Much better than *I* receive," I agreed, "either here or as the teacher of the old class!"

"You're not teaching now?" he said, after a pause.

"I became a little discouraged, I guess," I told him. "A teacher's pay is so low, so hard to live on. I have a child to raise, too, you know. Then, sometimes I get the idea I'm not doing much of anything really. Superiors sometimes tell me I see so much more in my pupils than is really there. I'm a dreamer, they say, seeing things that *aren't*."

"Of course," he said, "I wouldn't know about that. It's not likely that I'll ever be a school teacher. But before I go—and I'm glad we finally got together—for a long time I've been wanting to tell you this: without you I'd never be the success I am; and I *am* a success, Mrs. Smith."

"I am so well aware of that, Paul."

We shook hands. He turned and was gone. I did not see him again, but I saw his neat, correct reports right up to the time I turned my back on war work, on its higher pay, and returned to where I belonged, to work with the retarded.

It was not long after Paul and I met, either.

Something he said made me eager to go back to my real work, where I was happiest, possibly because that war—against ignorance, stupidity, cruelty, and fear—is the one war in all the world that will not end while men inhabit the earth.

XXI

The Simple Things

I HAVE accented reading in this homely tale of "Mrs. Smith's Class." It should be understood that geography, arithmetic, spelling, history, and the other usual academic subjects are also taught. I accent reading because without it there is no progress in anything else. Take care of a child's reading, establish its level at the highest possible point for the individual, and the rest eventuates as a matter of course. The whole technique is simple.

I have a conviction that educators make the education of the retarded seem too difficult. The simplest activity can be made difficult—so that only a qualified expert can manage it—if someone wishes to make it so, and has the vocabulary to accomplish results.

There are many books, hundreds, which set forth the proper, accepted techniques of special education of the retarded. They take extra expense for granted.

There need be little extra expense, except here: I teach eighteen pupils, which I regard as the manageable norm. Teachers of normal classes teach twice as many, or more. But I must teach my pupils as individuals as well as in a class group. I must find time for each pupil. Here is the key. Jesus provided it when he said, "Suffer the little children to come unto me." The teacher suffers little children to come unto her. She makes herself available, never formidable, never authoritative. This is not spoiling the child, but saving it, rehabilitating it.

There is a mistaken theory among some teachers that the child with an I.Q. of less than 90, down to 50, can make progress only through the fourth grade reading level. I do not accept this. Many of my pupils have progressed to the sixth grade, some have returned to regular classes and gone on during school age. While some subjects are impossible to learn after the sixth grade, others are not.

Retarded children have one thing in common: they are slow learners. But each has something individual which accentuates his lack of ability to learn. This I must find. The obvious things are taken care of before the child enters my class, or shortly afterward. He has a careful physical check-up, his hearing, vision, teeth are all studied for keys to comprehension.

There is always, in my experience, some easily discovered landmark to the retarded. Maybe it is a lisp, stammering, sullen withdrawal. It may vary with each individual so far that there is no comparison, save in the common denominator of slowness.

I know it is useless to hunt for some pattern, in some book, into which I can comfortably fit any retarded child, and then spoon-feed him into rehabilitation. I cannot reiterate too often: the slow child must be taught as an individual until he can move alone with the confidence of the normal child.

Every child with an I.Q. of 50 or above, barring physical defects undiscovered or impossible of correction, can and must be rehabilitated.

To teach the slow child nimble use of hands and feet, at the expense of his mind, is criminal.

Actually, the simple individual technique by which any child can and must be rehabilitated should begin at home. But few parents, while they must teach whether or not they are qualified, are actually teachers; so the teacher of the retarded must take the place of the parent. One drawback is that the child has already retreated into his personal sanctuary when he reaches the special class, and must be recalled. This recall is the task of the teacher.

And it is actually as simple as standing at a door and calling:

"Come here, let us talk together."

It is finding the door which is closed upon difficulties, for the slow naturally and automatically hides and camouflages his personal door. He does not wish his privacy to be invaded. Nor does the teacher invade it. She invites the child forth. It is not easy to find words to make this technique clear, since the door is not always easy to find, *but it is always there.*

I am convinced that it is also always there in the child called "severely retarded." I cite Carol as my prize example, though I have not enough examples to establish proof, or indicate a technique. But how many Carols do we have to find before we become aware that "lost sheep" are slipping through our fingers, to be lost throughout their lives? Without sentimentality, think of these "lost sheep," numbering in the tens of thousands in a given school year, nationally, as having to be fed and housed at the taxpayer's expense. The tax bill is enormous.

And it need not be. It is expensive only because the task is made to look difficult, and because we place so much emphasis on expensive handicrafts. Simple, practical crafts which fit the needs of everyday life are far more satisfactory. They help the child in his later life, for they give him the experience to meet and handle daily home needs. Building the mind and body, grooming the personality, and shaping the moral trend of his mind, these cost approximately the same as the regular classes.

The expense of special education then is largely vested in equipment and supplies *intended for the use of the hands*. This need not be.

Actual requirements, which I have proved year after year, are these: the pupil in person, the teacher in person constantly, the classroom, and exactly such supplies as are normally needed in graded classes. The answer is not gadgetry of any nature, though I do believe that slow children should have the manual training available to normal pupils —and no more unless they desire it so obviously that it indicates their bent. For the close rapport between teacher and pupil, pupils and pupil, class and teacher, class and individuals, *the equipment is almost entirely human.*

The teacher has within her brain, if she is qualified at all, all she needs to rehabilitate a slow child—with ordinary school supplies added: paper, pencils, blackboards, books, bulletin boards, desks, the appurtenances of the average modern classroom in any elementary school. One major expense is necessary: the cost of small classes.

Yet, taking taxes into consideration, which is more expensive: to provide twice as many teachers for the slow, or to let them grow up, more or less willy-nilly, more or less footballs, and lock them up when they break the law, or pay their personal expenses during their lives?

I could suggest that the special education teacher double

in brass to keep down expenses; that she teach a normal class while she teaches a class of the slow, but this is out of the question. *The slow learner requires the teacher's full time during school hours.* These hours may sometimes extend through a twenty-four-hour period, for the teacher must spend time pondering on her work for tomorrow. All teachers do this, but teachers of the normal have established techniques that, approximately, work. The teacher of the special class has intuition, and a knack for perception of the slow, and she often requires extra time to invoke this inner technique.

Once the key has been found, the child should not be hurried. There should be no pressure, no compulsion. Discipline, yes, but pressure, no. Not until the ability to withstand pressure has been encouraged to the utmost in the retarded child, is that child capable of combatting even implied pressure. The child requires help, not rehabilitation via a funnel, through a set maze, via a pattern, out of standardized books. The reason is simple: the slow child is standardized in his slowness only; the rest is individual, as much that child's own as his fingerprints.

My techniques are so simple that, possibly, they should not even be called techniques. Comparatively few of them are solely mine. All have been used, but I do not *mis*use them, or bend the child's neck to fit them; I fit them to the child.

If I had one wish and believed it could be granted, it would be this: that I could have retarded children, not at the age of eight or nine, but from the moment medical science could establish their approximate I.Q.

In at least one place in the United States an experiment is under way to see the effect of beginning the training and education of these children at nursery age, thus pre-educating them to their later needs. It seems impossible, but I am not at all sure that is not the way.

I think, "Maybe, if there were a book about it . . ." Then I think on, "Heaven forbid, for have I not said repeatedly that it is not found in books?" It is, of course, found in books, but not in published books. It is found in each slow child's personal book of life. That is what I must be able to read, and teach its owner to read.

Possibly a general book might provide the master key to all those little books of life.

Meanwhile, hints on which any teacher can proceed, follow.

XXII

Prelude to the Circus

ONE YEAR I took my class to the circus. It was more, for all of us, than just a journey to entertainment. I turn everything into educational channels. How better could I learn the inner self of my charges than by seeing them as they looked at dramatic activities which since the first circus have appealed to old and young alike? To slow and normal alike?

How did these retarded children react?

Exactly as individuals at every I.Q. level react! And that again is the key to whatever technique I may be said to have.

Not one of my pupils failed to laugh at the clowns. And clowns paused before us to make sure we did react. They picked us out because we were teacher and pupils, not because we were retarded. I checked with each of my children on many items. Did they laugh at the same thing normal people did? Did they laugh at noses all out of proportion to faces? They did. They noticed that the noses of the clowns were usually red, the cheeks white, the lips painted and big-looking—and these things, so out of proportion, were funny to every child. Nor did one laugh, I am sure, because the others did.

"Is the clown funny, Bette?" I would ask.

"Oh, yes, *very* funny."

"What makes him funny?"

"He uses such a big rope to lead such a small dog!"

"How else is he funny?"

"His clothes are so baggy. They're not like anybody's clothes except the clothes of other clowns. He flops around in them."

Bette does not yet speak too fluently, but I have no difficulty in understanding her.

"And how many clowns are there? Count on your fingers if that makes it easier."

"There are seven clowns," she said correctly. I could use many items in the circus for arithmetic problems, as far as Bette was concerned. And if for her, for the others.

I knew in advance, of course, that there would be elephants at the circus, so my pupils all carried either flash cards or paper on which the word "elephant" was printed. I could make all sorts of use of such cards. I could write on each card, beforehand: "how many elephants are there?" I could write on another piece of paper not only "what color is the elephant?" but "how many different colors do you see at the circus?"

"Where does the elephant come from?" is another simple question for the more advanced retarded, meaning one who has been with me long enough to read well and have a background of geography. This geographical background is utilized in recognizing and commenting on all the animals, birds, and reptiles we see at the circus.

Of course there is one thing I must guard against: some of my pupils may be adversely affected by snakes, snarling lions, or leopards, so I watch closely. I also explain, if any become afraid, that the cages are secure; no animals can escape and do them any harm. I pray, at the same time, that what I say proves to be the truth! If an animal escapes I am undone, proved not reliable!

But none escaped. While listening to the comments of the children, and enjoying the elephants, the trained horses, the trapeze artists, the band, the seals, the ringmaster, the cowboys, the dogs, ducks, geese, clowns, ornate wagons, the Big Top—all the exciting things that make up the circus—I was planning simple use to make of every conceivable item. As an idea came to me I jotted it down.

Doubtless some of my notes will seem silly to anybody who reads them: as silly, in fact, as so many thoughtless parents and teachers and adults generally regard the questions of childhood.

"Mama, why does the elephant have such big ears? Mama, what are the elephants' big teeth made of? Papa, why is a clown? Papa, could *I* ride a horse standing up like that?"

While I watched, and while I made notes, one of my children after the other came to me with questions like those above:

"Mrs. Smith, what makes an elephant so *big*? How much do you suppose that baby elephant weighs?"

I tell him what I can remember about elephants. I also tell him I do not know, if I don't, and that he is to remind me of his question when we get back to school, today or tomorrow, so we can look up the answer together. I would be foolish to pretend knowledge I do not possess, or do not remember. I would be a liar, and children quickly lose faith in liars. I would be worse than a liar if, to cover up the gaps in poor memory, or lack of knowledge, I put the child off with this:

"Don't ask silly questions! Let *me* enjoy the circus, too!"

We may indulge some guessing as to the weight of the

baby elephant. I may guess that it weighs a ton, or that its mother weighs two tons. Then my questioner is sure to ask, "how many of something is a ton?" in order to reduce the elephant's size to something he can grasp. And he can grasp it at least as nearly as I myself can, since I am not much at home with elephants, even academically. I shall lose nothing personal by being honest with my pupils, for what I lose I shall more than make up for tomorrow, when we really begin to make use of the circus. Anyway, if my questioner learns nothing else, he learns that a big elephant may weigh "tons," and he may have learned a new word. If he has learned nothing else, the circus has paid for itself for that child. *Any progress the slow child makes is worth its weight in educators and the patience the teacher may have to exercise.*

I could arrange to buy popcorn and candy, or soft drinks, but the children are self-reliant, or wish to be. They bring with them their admission fee and some spending money if they can afford it. If not I manage it somehow. Here is an excellent place to learn to buy, pay, make change, and know when proper change is returned. I have heard, as have most people, of short-change artists at fairs and circuses, but have not myself experienced them. I even doubt their existence. I do not tell the children about such characters. They most likely do not exist, and would not stoop to cheating children if they did. I show the class how to make change before we go to the circus. I may spend a day or two on this—a fine chance for some simple but effective arithmetic. Then, each child buys his own ticket. If I buy tickets for my children it makes them "babies," which not even normal children like!

My children have spending money from five cents to fifty

cents. I find it expedient to limit spending money, when they bring their own. I will not cause the child whose people can ill afford a dime to be jealous of the child who can afford a dollar. And if the child who has a half dollar wishes to buy for and treat schoolmates, I certainly do not discourage him, or her. Later I talk about it back in the classroom, to make sure that the child's generosity is recognized.

We buy programs enough to remember and to take back to the classroom for study activities. There are so many new words in a program that it can serve almost as a supplementary reader, and words learned are valuable words, regardless of where they are printed. There are pictures, too, which may later be used to remind my pupils that the elephant did in fact have big ears, tusks, a trunk, a small tail. Everything is grist to the mill.

I do not limit myself to what the school provides, though I can successfully do so. By switching to something that does not have "school" written into its shape and size, I continue to school my pupils almost without their knowledge. I hasten to add that it is never without their knowledge, for no child is quicker than the retarded child to know when he is being painlessly educated; he rather likes it painless!

"What makes the dwarf so little?" a girl asks.

"How big is this tent?"

"What is a sideshow?"

"What's the name of that big thing on the wagon that makes music?" This child refers to the calliope, which takes a bit of explaining. Every child has fun mastering the new word. Is it a valuable word? Will the child ever use it again? It is a valuable word. The child may never use it again, possibly even when he goes to the circus next time. But whenever he hears the word he will be reminded of the circus *and much of what he learned there,* when he was so happy and laughing.

"Why do some horses have white hair, some other colors?"

This can be a poser, but I confess that, knowing my children, I have prepared to some extent for unexpected questions. I cannot explain to a small child, fully and scientifically, why one horse is white, another black, another bay. But I can tell him within his range of acceptance, and when I have done so he knows much more about shapes, sizes, colors, tints, shades. He knows what is "large," what is "small," that one animal has four legs and four feet while a man has but two.

It is easy to turn the circus into a classroom, without its seeming to be one, simply because the children enjoy it so much; and because joys are easily remembered, the young are likely to remember little items connected with their joys: like "calliope," which Bette could not pronounce but to which she listened, so enthralled that she will never forget the musical gadget.

Children are fascinated by heights. They gasp when the troupe performs on the high wire without a net, and I find it necessary to explain that this cannot be done without careful training, since I wish none of my pupils to experiment with wires too high, and not tight enough. They pop their eyes and gape their mouths when trapeze performers do their death-defying tricks. If there is anything retarded in their reactions here, I do not see it. Even the vacuous-faced boy becomes animated and eager, proving to me what I have suspected all along, that he has found that vacuity somehow pays him. I can be wrong, but I am working on him, knowing with every fresh glimpse of him that I will reach him.

"Why do they wear tights?"

Of course they ask this after they have asked questions whose answers must include the word "tights." This may not be one of the words I particularly want a boy or girl to remember, but if it is new, and he learns it, he has widened his capacity for retention.

"Why do they have sawdust in the ring?"

"What kind of monkeys are those?"

"Why does a leopard have spots, a tiger stripes?"

"Why are they called big cats? Are they anything like our small cats?"

"Where do circuses come from? Where do they go?"

"Can I ever be in a circus?"

"What is a giant? What *makes* him a giant?"

All these questions must be answered honestly, and correctly, if the teacher knows the answers. I may make all the preparation of which I can conceive, studying for days in advance of the circus, to be able to answer questions, and my class will almost certainly surprise me with questions I could never possibly previse.

"What kind of wood does the sawdust come from?"

It should be obvious that I can make a great deal of that question, while I can maintain interest in it. It may well lead to a visit by the class to the nearest sawmill, and then to the nearest woods where trees can be more accurately discussed.

"Where do circus people come from? Where are dwarfs born? Giants? Indians?"

I can be busy, when they ask me questions, interpolating questions of my own.

"Circus people come from all over the world," I may say. "That applies to dwarfs, too. And how many dwarfs do you see, John? How many giants? Have you counted the horses?"

I can be busy, *and if I am doing my duty I am as busy as I can possibly be.*

So that's what happened that trip; not all that happened, not by a great deal. Many more questions were asked than I have indicated. I tried to answer them all. I was answering them in my dreams that night and, I doubt not, in their dreams all my children were still asking them—after virtually exhausting their parents between return from the circus and bedtime.

I came away from the circus with a sheaf of papers on which I had written certain small items. I made plans for these items as I went along. I knew, when I wrote something on a piece of paper, just who would receive that paper today, and was careful not to write beyond his, or her, ability to read—*or to learn to read today.*

My children knew, because we have visited other areas of interest than the circus, that they would hear about the circus again. They will not mind. Making them remember will not be work at all, but a continuation of the circus itself, which every last one of them enjoyed.

From the circus they have already learned much and will learn more today and tomorrow. While we concentrate on the circus, we will learn more of reading, spelling, arithmetic—even fractions!—geography, history, current events, colors, sounds, music, natural laws, social behavior, than any one of them would believe possible. When I show them, soon, what they learned—and I make it my business to show them, unforgettably—they find it difficult to believe. But, and this is the truly important part, they are proud that they have learned new things—*so easily and painlessly!*

Now, it is time to do something with my notes, on those big pieces of paper. I have printed my simple observations, so that even my almost-non-readers can understand, or can be shown by their schoolmates.

They call what I next do a "project," and so it is, but when my pupils and I finish with a project, all of us together defy anyone else to squeeze anything out of what we have left unused.

In our class the project, by some regarded as foolish, comes completely into its own, to prove that nothing by which men learn is really foolish. If it produces results, it will always prove satisfactory and worth while.

One warning: make the goal marked "satisfactory" one not quickly or easily attained. When a project, pattern, day, bulletin, event, is wasted in whole or in part, it is not the project, pattern, day, bulletin, or event that matters, but the innerself of the child, who has been cheated of what he might have learned.

Even if a child forgets what he has learned—and the retarded are not famous for retentiveness—he can learn other things, and recall that thing he did learn without too great difficulty. *He is getting practice at learning.*

Who else gets more out of any activity?

I select boys and girls to distribute my bits of paper. I may deliberately select a boy who cannot resist the temptation to read papers before he passes them out. He reads:

"We are going to the circus. This is the big tent. This is where we go in."

Of course there is nothing on the paper but my printed words. I need scarcely tell the boy or girl who receives that piece of paper that he is expected to fill the blank space.

I have other notes from yesterday on other pieces of paper, for other boys and girls.

There is much blank space to fill. I know I have their attention when I explain to them what I expect them to do about filling those blank spaces.

They have already discovered that my notes are printed on drawing paper.

They can scarcely wait for me to cause the colored crayons to be distributed.

XXIII

The Book Builders

MOST of the books in my classroom are made to stand stresses. Children require time in which to develop the delicate touch. Their hands are naturally heavy.

I lift a book, almost any book, from the class library.

"What is it?" I ask.

"Book."

"Notice," I say, "how the book is put together. These are pages. These are words, paragraphs, sentences, on the pages. These are illustrations. This is the binding. This is the jacket. Notice that this binding has a firm design; that this jacket is a kind of picture. Notice that the pages are numbered. Notice that the book is separated into chapters. This back is part of the binding. This back part of the book, opposite where it opens, is the backbone. Does this book interest you?"

"Yes!"

"Do you have any idea how it is made?"

Silence. They have never visited a printing or binding establishment connected with publishing.

"Do you think you could study the books in this classroom, and then select one of them as the one you could copy?"

"Oh, yes!"

"Good!" I say. "Then we are going to make a book of our own. Most of our names will be in it, just as there is a name, and are sometimes many names, in printed books. We are not machines, so we shall make our book by hand. We are efficient boys and girls, however, so we shall make everything that goes into the construction of a book. First, these brown, thick sheets on which I have made certain marks, are to be the pages of our book. In order for our binding to cover the outside of our book, consisting of many pages, must the binding be larger or smaller?"

"Larger!" calls out Peter.

"Smawer!" cries Carol. Then she corrects herself, "No, bigger!"

"What shall we use to fasten the sheets to the binding?"

"String! Paste! Nails! Screws!"

We settle for string, stouter than shoestring, because every boy and girl knows that shoestrings break, usually when they are in a hurry to reach school, or to get home from school.

We organize a work group to measure a blank sheet which is exactly the size of the brown paper I am using for pages. I am not going to mind if their judgment is bad in the matter of size. Retarded children are not expected to be bookbinders or publishers to delight some rich purchaser. It is enough for me that the size resulting is approximately right —improvement will come gradually, as in every undertaking, even among the normal—and that my group fastens onto an idea and carries it through.

"Now, I'm going to pass out these pages. Each of you will read what I have printed on his page. He, or she, will do his best to draw what my printing suggests. If I suggest the circus tent, draw a circus tent. If it makes you think of a horse, or lion, or elephant, anywhere near the tent, draw that, too, as best you can. You will select your own colors. If you remember what the tent really did look like, what color it was, you may use that color, but you don't have to. Maybe you can draw a tent prettier than the circus tent itself!"

I pause to let that sink in.

"George, what does your paper say?"

George reads: "I am a clown. I am a funny clown, I like to laugh."

"Did you see a clown like that yesterday?"

"Yes."

"You can draw a clown, can't you?"

"I can draw more than one clown."

"But my printing does not say more than one clown."

"My sheet says," speaks up Peter, "that here are four clowns. I would rather draw one clown."

"If you and George would like to trade, you may."

"Why can't we work together on our clowns?"

"That's a fine idea. The better people work together the better they live. George and Peter may sit together, or pull their desks together, and help each other."

Some noise results, but it is industrious noise.

When I have explained all the sheets, I go a bit further.

"Now, you do the best you know how, and don't try to see who will finish first. All drawings will be pinned on the walls above the blackboards, so that everyone can see them, including visiting parents, visitors from other rooms, other teachers. . . ."

"Then can we write or print our names on what we draw?"

This is not a new idea. I have given them a sense of possession in the material things they make or symbolize in drawings. They have all seen illustrations, cartoons, comics, caricatures, signed by the illustrators.

"You *should* sign your work," I agree.

"What if I can't write or print my name?" asks the newest arrival.

"Then you make some mark on your paper," I say, "so that you will know it is yours. Later, you'll be able to print or sign your own name. Wouldn't it be nice if you could do it now?"

"Yeth."

"Maybe, because you wish you could do it now, you will try harder?"

"Yeth!"

"Then I'll print your name for you, just your Christian name, people call it your first name, or your given name, and you see if you can't draw the printing, just as you're going to draw a horse, an elephant, a burro, a mule, or a zebra. Can you do that? Of *course* you can!"

I expect no miracles of book-making or bookbinding. I divide my class into groups, each busy with some segment of manufacture. I have found through the years that an hour is about as long as a group of children, retarded or not, can maintain interest in a project. After that they are likely to scuffle, talk, rush about.

But I can do so much in an hour with the individuals who are not yet candidates for the joy of book-manufacture. I take those who must be left out because they have not yet gone far enough, and work with them at my own desk. I can lose myself in this work, assured that the groups before my desk require no discipline. Practice has conditioned me to sounds, and time. When sounds attract my attention, I raise my head to look upon certain disturbance in the class.

I quell it, or divert it somehow that seems appropriate. Too, I am like an alarm clock, or a cook's timing device. When the hour is up, or within a few minutes one way or the other, more likely shortly before the hour is up—since the slow, like the normal of all ages, are prone to watch the clock and "jump the gun," rather than work overtime—I raise my head, as certainly as a wound alarm clock goes off, or a timer rings a single bell.

We take a break of some kind, or we may put the book aside until tomorrow. But it is never forgotten, for the book must be finished, as a remembered example of good practice: finish whatever you start. Pupils always suggest, "let's do more work on the book," if I attempt to skip a day. If they choose work on the book because they prefer it, as easier, to some other project, it does not matter—*so long as they learn the items the project is designed to teach them.*

For example, a child may find the abstract "two plus two" somewhat difficult, but he can see—and by counting on his fingers prove—that two clowns plus two clowns add up to four clowns.

"Why," Gudrun asked me at the circus yesterday, "are the rings round?"

That provides me with more ammunition. A bit at a time I show them all, in drawing, the differences between a square, a circle, a rectangle, a triangle. I print the words. Then I draw—though I am not a very good artist—a clown standing on a circle, a square in front of another clown, a rectangle behind another clown, a triangle on another clown's head, like a hat. My more advanced pupils get pages of these shapes, and are told to write inside each figure what that figure is. Those who are right have their pages in our Book of the Circus, signed with their names.

More, less, big, little, larger, smaller, first, last, middle, over, under, behind, before . . .

I can use one of those words in every legend I choose to print on my pages of notes. My artists may have to ask me a dozen times, or a score of times, the difference between over, under, before, behind, but when interest is stimulated by something memorable, I do not mind if I have to answer each question scores of times. When it has finally "sunk in," my student has learned another small item which proves that, given time, opportunity, love, and understanding, he can master two, or three, or however many he may need in his life after school.

I never visit a place, an activity, an industry, a circus, with my class that I am not surprised by some of their questions, surprised that they see so much.

I may note, at the circus, guy ropes, tent pegs, cages, calliopes, the band's instruments, wires, swings, inverted buckets on which elephants stand, money, candy, popcorn, soft drinks, sawdust, tent flaps, doors, seats, benches, railings, rings, poles, flags, banners, harness. I may make notes to remind myself that I should waste nothing, that I should make sure that everything is used later, educationally, for the benefit of my pupils. I pride myself on the keenness and detail of my personal observation. I am sure that I miss nothing; yet always one or more of my eighteen pupils calls my attention to something I had not seen, or speaks of something, next day, that I did not see.

For instance: "Who made the merry-go-round?" I saw and heard the merry-go-round, of course, and most of my pupils rode, but I did not foresee that anybody would ask me who invented it. If I know, I tell; if I do not, we look it up, and I find a natural excuse for talking about inventions, and great American inventors.

One slow child of my reading acquaintance who, however, went to school before I was born, was the son of a slave. He graduated from the fourth grade. He reads slowly, diffidently. He hires the normal of two great races to help him manufacture his inventions. His gross income is $250,000 yearly. Is he exceptional? Only in degree.

Slowly, not hurrying, but wasting no time, we "print" and bind our Book of the Circus. One of my girls, one of my boys, at virtually the same time, conceive the idea that since jackets of our regularly printed books wear, tear, and vanish, we should illustrate the binding, rather than have an illustrated jacket.

Our binding becomes a futuristic design which any one of my proud pupils can explain eagerly to any visitor; and which all eighteen will volunteer to do with almost no encouragement!

Our book is finally printed, illustrated, bound; it is "published." It is not thrown away while one of its makers remains in the class. It is held until another book is attempted, whereupon it becomes an example.

"But of course," we say, "*we* can do better than this, can't we?"

"Yes, Mrs. Smith, a *lot* better!"

We can, too. Sometimes I am compelled, for lack of space, to discard one of my pupils' books. It is always a heart-tug.

XXIV

Towers of Ivory

No TEACHER can dwell apart from the community. This is especially true of the teacher of the retarded. The retarded, to be of any value to themselves and their community, must learn to fit into the community, more or less comfortably. They must fit at least as comfortably as any one else does. When the millennium arrives, everybody will be comfortable. Possibly, now, nobody is. So the human being of any age fits his niche only as comfortably as he can. That is the most the retarded can hope for. But this must be done: the retarded must be more carefully prepared to fit his niche approximately.

For that reason the teacher must know the community. No teacher worthy of the name can withdraw into the halls of knowledge, never emerge, and expect to succeed as a teacher or as a human being. The world of books has its compensations. Most of us yearn, at one time or another, to withdraw from the world, to live among books, paintings, the forests, on the mountains, and some of us may do it. Writers of "different" books may retire into ivory towers, and produce their books, successful in their own eyes.

The teacher who retires from the community ceases, the instant of withdrawal, to be a teacher. The more the teacher fits into the community, the greater his success as a teacher.

But there is a way to join the life of the community. One must take care, at the outset, not to waste one's time, or allow the community to waste it. It is sometimes the belief of non-teachers that the teacher works short hours, that after hours he has nothing to do but make himself available to the community in whatever way he is asked. The teacher is paid by the community, therefore the teacher owes the community all of his time.

To a large extent this is true; but the teacher owes his time to his pupils. And he spends more time for his pupils than, professionally, he spends with them.

The teacher must keep abreast of the times. He must know his community as no other member of the community knows it. No other member of the community, save other teachers, needs to know where the niches are, their size and shape, into which pupils are to be fitted. The teacher should be able to discuss newspapers with newspapermen, farms with farmers, libraries with librarians, the YMCA and YWCA with any people who are in any way interested in the YMCA and YWCA. And the teacher must discuss these matters authoritatively. The community expects, and rightly I think, that the teacher shall know.

The teacher owes it to his pupils to know.

The teacher lives somewhere, in an apartment, the YMCA, a private residence, with the parents of school-children, so he should know his neighbors, *but never under any circumstances should he discuss them anywhere, with anybody*. While the community may interest itself in the scholastic attainments of its children but little, it holds its teachers strictly accountable. Few people in public life are so vulnerable. Whatever they say or do not say is weighed and balanced.

And this is as it should be, though so often it seems, to the teachers themselves, to be unfair. But the teacher who cannot fit into his community is not likely to be able to fit anyone else into it. The proper study of the teacher is his community, not next after, but currently with, his pupils.

No teacher, not even the genius, can know his community by withdrawing from it. He can learn it, and know more about it than anyone else in it, only by reading it, smelling it, hearing it, touching it, sharing it, as no other professional is ever likely to do.

I have said that I do not research the parents of my pupils, since I recognize the normal weakness of my humanity, and am afraid I may allow myself to be prejudiced. I am as sensitive as anyone to ignorance, brutality, sloth, penury, greed, selfishness, and if I find these things in the parents of my pupils, I may excuse my pupils more than they should be excused. I may pity them when pity is an excuse. It never has any real value—compassion is proper enough, since it implies understanding—but I may in some fashion allow my personal feelings to make me less the teacher.

Yet those parents are members of the community. Maybe they are square pegs in round holes. Maybe they do not fit in anywhere. Maybe . . .

I make it my business to know what I need to know. I reserve judgment always. I do not find this easy to do, for I, like every other teacher, am plagued by my humanity. I must learn to make it work for me, for my pupils, for my community—and any community is mine into which I am thrown in the role of teacher.

I do not gossip. I give no one a chance to accuse me of gossiping. Therefore I dare not listen to gossip. It is too easy for someone who had told me something secret about someone else, something reprehensible (what else is gossip-worthy?), to say to a third party:

"Guess who just told me the *awfullest* thing about that Hester Lowery? . . ."

Of course, the habitual gossip may say that, though she may never even have talked with me or to me, but I can protect myself in every possible way. I can do this by refusing to be frivolous. I must do it without being so serious my community will be bored with me.

As a teacher I am always, whether or not I wish it, in some kind of spotlight. The guns of someone are always trained on me. Someone visits my class, and a Theodore seizes that opportunity to throw a tantrum. It is not Theodore or his parents who are blamed, but me—and rightly! Unless Theodore is new in my class, within a week of his joining, I am responsible for his behavior. If he fails me, fails the class, fails himself, the failure is mine. I become a subject of derogation as soon as that parent leaves my classroom. If the parent takes a child out of my schoolroom, because of something I have done or have not done, I am virtually undone.

I can escape all this, of course, by crawling into my classroom and staying there. I can go to my room at night and stay there. I can go out after dinner, so long as I do not stay so late I create suspicion. I can travel certain streets, to and from work, to and from stores, libraries, other interests tied in with my work as a teacher. I can do these things, and never, though I spend all my life in that community, become a part of my community. How, then, can I hope to make even the most nearly normal of my pupils a member of that community?

There are activities in which I must participate. I must

select them with the utmost care. Some will select me, but
this may not be fortunate. Some may select me because someone else who should be doing that job evades his responsibility, and the job is handed to me. This I must not allow.
I must be firm about it. I must explain, so that none will
accuse me, honestly, of evading my duty to the community
which pays my salary.

And that that salary is small is no excuse whatever for
failure on my part. I knew when I became a teacher that I
should never be rich. If I had been ambitious for wealth, I
would never have become a teacher.

I became a teacher for a number of reasons, the most important being that I wished to help humanity, retarded
humanity in my case, find itself in this chaotic world. I can
help the retarded child to find himself only when I know
where I myself am, with relation to myself, my pupils, my
community.

Educators as a whole are prone to stand too much apart
from their environment. They show up on special occasions,
like the groundhog, and their own neighbors are often surprised to realize that they and their educators are practically
unknown to one another. It is not enough that an educator
contact his community on special days, like Commencement,
or that he write books instructing the community how it
should behave toward its children and their educators—
especially their educators!—or that he make periodic public appearances on radio or television.

The educator, of whatever rank—and he should not be too
conscious of his rank, his degrees, his I.Q—who is a misfit
in his community, is a misfit in his home, in his school, and
the best he can do with his pupils is to make them misfits,
too. Of course, many pupils become good citizens, successful

in spite of their teachers, but most pupils, even those who all their school lives violently disapprove of their teachers, take their educators as examples. Next to their own parents, whom else have they?

One never becomes a good example by hiding.

There are no legitimate ivory towers for the efficient teacher.

XXV

Who Come Before Me

I HAVE lost four pupils in fifteen years. Their parents, whose influence was greater than mine, would not let me have them. Four teen-age boys, because their parents said that "Mrs. Smith's Class" was a disgrace and a waste of time—they meant that their children were disgraced, and thus disgraced their family, by being sent to a special class—refused to learn anything. They could have learned.

Every child with an I.Q. of 50 or above, and possibly with I.Q.'s considerably below 50, can be rehabilitated. I can rehabilitate every such child I can reach. Tragically, I can reach but eighteen each year, and give each one that personal attention he needs. Such children should come to me, and teachers like me, by the time they are six, surely by the time they are eight. I can reach older ones, but the difficulties become greater with each passing year, month, week, even day.

And why is this?

Frankly, parents, neighbors, playmates.

Parents do not always accept their responsibilities. They can carry out their responsibilities easily enough, and they should—or brand themselves criminals in some degree—if they will disregard the weight of a little personal work.

Children ask questions all day long. Retarded children probably ask more questions because they are slower to understand. If they do not ask questions the danger is obvious, the work of destruction already begun. They have, finding themselves different, started crawling into themselves to hide.

Whether or not parents want children when they are conceived, when such children come into the world, those who conceived them are responsible for them. The state takes over some of the responsibility when children are six, seven, or eight, provided their I.Q. is 50 or above. Yet those first six, seven, or eight years are the most important in the life of the child. As the child is father of the man, so the baby, the toddler, the runner, the chance-taker, the pre-primer child, is father of the kindergarden child. And *his* father is his first teacher. So is his mother. How the parents play their roles, each parent must decide for himself, bearing this in mind:

No child whose mind works at all is uneducable, within limits that are not nearly as well defined, as yet, as they will be some day, after constant research. I have seen "vegetable" children become lovable, thinking children, because I loved them and helped them to think.

I have so many times wished I could start with all my children when they first start talking, before they have learned that they are different. This is not egotistical. It is just that I see, and teach, and rehabilitate more slow learners than any parent ever has, or experiences. And I devote all my time to them, study them from all angles, something that parents are unable, or feel themselves unable, to do.

Parents must give more thought to their slow children, and that means more time. While doing it they must concentrate not on coddling the retarded, offering themselves as crutches, but on showing the retarded, and proving to them, that their minds, while slow, are just as good as those of faster-acting friends, relatives, playmates.

No question any child can ask a father or mother should go unanswered. This is especially true of the slow learner, whom father and mother should be able to recognize when or before the child begins talking. To lack patience with small questioners is to admit oneself retarded emotionally. Let us face that fact, and never again be tempted to impatience.

When a child asks a parent a question which the parent cannot answer, or does not have time to answer, no answer at all is better than an impatient one—so long as, as soon as possible, the question *is* answered. To children, parents are Deity, protection, security, adults who never make mistakes. A parent caught in a mistake loses a child's respect, and growing fear takes its place. If the parent cannot be relied upon, how can strangers be? How can the slow hope to find safety anywhere in the world?

Children are sent to us parents in trust, that we may guide them to maturity. With the exception of the cowbird, virtually every parent in the animal kingdom guards, protects, feeds, and guides its offspring until it can fly, run, walk, swim, or slide on its own. And even the cowbird provides for its young by laying eggs in the nests of other birds.

Human parents are not cowbirds. Teachers and schools are not the nests of other birds. If they are so considered, bird-children should be sent to those nests at birth. This is ridiculous, of course, and put in here just to make readers remember.

Let the child follow about, asking questions. Answer

them, if you can. If you cannot, tell the child that you and he, together, will go hunting the answer as soon as possible. And do not put him off, hoping he will forget, for though retention is the major problem of the retarded, he will not forget an evasion on the part of those whom he regards as infallible. Make sure that the child has a proper, exhaustive answer to every question. Parents urge their children to save pennies, nickels, dimes; they provide piggy-banks for their offspring. But the offspring are themselves the most comprehensive, valuable piggy-banks that parents can find. Plant a question and answer in a child, and character and personality grow out of them. Deny the answer to a question and you rob the bank; but you do more than merely rob the bank; you, in part, destroy it. You destroy it by attacking its weakest, most vulnerable, point: its youth, its defenselessness.

Many parents would be horrified at the idea of "knocking some sense" into their child's head. They regard corporal punishment as criminal. Yet they use techniques much more harmful than knocks of any merely physical kind. They hit a child with impatient words, or feint with frowns and withhold the words the child has every right to expect.

To fail a child is to fail in one's part in man's evolution. Man, of all creatures, knows his function in evolution. If he does not exercise it, he has no right to the niche he has usurped. Part of his evolution is to provide footholds, handholds, on evolution's ladder, for the young. To make his place less controversial, he is expected to provide only for his own young. Surely, as he was provided for in his childhood, he should repay nature by providing for his own children. If, in his youth, father was not provided for, then his knowledge of his childhood lacks should make his responsi-

bility to his own all the clearer. Mother, too; for mothers, as
well as fathers and other relatives, have times of impatience,
of self-pity, of feeling put-upon.

There is no time, ever, not to pay heed to the child. Discipline is the great neglected necessity in our western world.
None knows this better than the teacher to whom the children are sent—by relieved, thankful parents—when they
are old enough. But discipline, with the naturally shy, more-
than-average slow, child, must be tempered with that justice
and love and understanding which every parent believes he
has, yet so comparatively few have the patience to utilize.

Talking proper training for the retarded child has its
place. Unfortunately, the child himself does not understand
educational theories and techniques when he hears them
discussed learnedly by adults. The slow child, eavesdrop-
ping, may know he is being discussed, that he is a problem,
but he knows beyond that only what his parents tell him.

If they tell him little, nothing, or incorrect facts, his confusion is a numbing, deadening result. When evasions are
constantly repeated, by the time the child reaches school his
habits of spiritual withdrawal have become so nearly fixed
that only the patient, knowing teacher can ferret out his
sanctuary and bring him forth.

I am prone to believe that parents of retarded children,
doing their simple duty by those children, can virtually, in
time, wipe out some of the need for rehabilitation in a class
like mine. There will always be a need for a specialized
program of education, however, to fit the demands of the
slower mind.

This is my real cry in the wilderness; that parents of slow
children—who must surely know, early in their children's
lives, that the children are slow—not withhold themselves

from their children against the time when all responsibility can be piled on the shoulders of a teacher of the retarded.

That this same suggestion applies to normal children may be true; but normal children have naturally a better chance to find their own way, even if they do not start school until eight years of age, than has the child who loses his courage, knowing himself different, before he even knows the difference between courage and cowardice.

I feel free to plead with parents, because I know parents; I am a parent. Though my child is not retarded, I could not love her less, or be less sympathetic with her, if she were. Indeed, I should love her more, give her more of my time—if that were possible—than I do now. That she is self-reliant, that she makes fewer demands on me than she would if she were slow, does not alter the simple fact of my responsibility.

I see a passing parent of a slow child and, knowing, I look after her. Do I pity her because she could so easily be I? Not at all! The Father, I firmly believe, as I have already said here, trusts most highly those to whom He sends His small slow ones.

Parents simply cannot betray that trust.

It should be understood, before I close the door of this, my classroom, that these children, with one exception, are not those found in my class today. Neither were they in one class at any one time. I have taught children from seven to seventeen during my years of experience, and their I.Q.'s have ranged from 50 to 89.

At the present time, however, I am most fortunate. My class has a range of I.Q.'s from 50 to 75 and an age range of eight to ten, which is as it should be. Because of the age of the children, we are placed inconspicuously in an elementary school. In the past I have had boys and girls from eight to fifteen years of age in the same class. Their I.Q.'s ranged from 50 to 89. The variance of I.Q.'s could have been handled with no more difficulty than that found in any heterogeneous class. The variance of age, however, presented numerous undesirable problems, for the handling of such a hodge-podge is not only difficult for the teacher, it also makes complete rehabilitation impossible for the more severe cases. I have found it impossible to handle competently boys and girls of fifteen with others aged eight in the same unit. The emotional, mental, and physical difference is too great. This is true even when there is only one sex involved. A group of widely divergent ages counteracts rehabilitative measures and adds new problems, many of which are sex and behavior problems.

It is impossible to mold a child's character properly when, in the same room or in the same building, there are gangs of older teen age "hero" leaders whose sole intent is to show power over the young. These are some of the factors which handicap the present handling of retarded pupils.

It is my hope that we, as educators, will someday see to it that these children come to specially trained teachers before they become frustrated by continued failure. Preventative action could remove to a great extent emotional and behavior problems.

We must get these children while they are young enough for us to mold their character and their minds. We must get them before they feel themselves misfits. We must see that they are not segregated or stigmatized. Stigmatization will always follow classes used as a dumping ground for all ages. Stigmatization will always follow over-age children kept in a school from which they ordinarily would have been promoted. Stigmatization will always follow pupils whose lot it is to be in a school in which some or all of the faculty segregate them by manner and tone.

These are some of the things we must change in the schools themselves. In so doing we will be well compensated because we will have opened for these boys and girls a new world. We will have set their feet on the path toward good citizenship and a happy, healthful, participating life.

The general public likewise must lend an understanding hand to these children and be willing to share in the responsibility of seeing that they are educated properly.

This is not an undertaking for parent alone, nor for school alone. It is a joint enterprise to which home, school, and community must contribute. These children ask so little. It is our joint responsibility to help them rise from ignorance and frustration to a life of purpose and productivity.

Index

Set in Linotype Granjon
Format by John Rynerson
Manufactured by the Haddon Craftsmen, Inc.
Published by HARPER & BROTHERS, *New York*